FREEDOM'S JUST ANOTHER WORD

BY DAN HAYS

"Freedom's Just Another Word," by Dan L. Hays. ISBN 978-1-60264-214-0 (soft) 978-1-60264-216-4 (hard).

Published 2008 by Virtualbookworm.com Publishing Inc., P.O. Box 9949, College Station, TX 77842, US. ©2008, Dan L. Hays. All rights reserved. No part of this publication may be reproduced, stored in a retrieval system, or transmitted in any form or by any means, electronic, mechanical, recording or otherwise, without the prior written permission of Dan L. Hays.

Manufactured in the United States of America.

My deepest thanks to the many people who believed in me when I couldn't believe in myself.

Karen, thanks for all your help, support and intuition along the way.

Joan, thanks for starting the whole thing by encouraging me to write.

Bob Kizer, thanks for teaching me how to release the past.

This book is dedicated to my Dad, who persevered against long odds, showing me the
way.

Chapter 1

I t was an overcast day in the middle of October in 1987. The Houston humidity was high, the air outside felt muggy, dense. To me, it felt like there was a shortage of air. I kept trying to catch my breath as I pulled up to the office building in the Memorial area. I sat in my car for a few minutes, trying to calm down as I watched a landscape crew trim the grass, probably for the last time that season, and rake the leaves starting to fall from the trees going dormant for winter.

I was going to ask for help. It was a big deal—I didn't do it often. While I was the guy who helped all my friends move into new apartments or houses, when I had to move I did it all by myself. So I wouldn't have to ask for help. Yet I was backed into a corner now, and had finally admitted I needed help. I'd been going through a time of paradoxes. Amazing growth and awareness intermingled with deep hopelessness and dreams of someone trying to hurt me. Feeling very free, yet trapped by my struggles to connect with the right job, feeling like I was somehow pulling myself away from jobs for a reason I could not fathom. I had been seeing a whole new connection with my Dad, and yet that very closeness and comfort with my Dad was inexplicably terrifying. I had written in my journal that I was either on a very powerful faith journey, or going crazy. I couldn't determine which it was. So I was going for counsel and aid to one of my spiritual mentors, a man to whom I had given a lot of credibility as a source of enlightenment; someone who had guided me and a lot of my friends in the past. Wayne had been a semi-regular speaker at our singles Sunday school class. He had taught Bible studies and led retreats for our group. He was charismatic, wealthy and successful, and we all admired him greatly. If anyone could shed light on my current situation, Wayne could. I had determined I needed to be honest with him about all my circumstances and ask for some financial help until I could get all of this sorted out. Wayne had recently helped one of my friends with a loan; I thought he would do so for me as well. I had thought about it for several weeks before approaching Wayne—was this the right thing to do, asking for his help—or should I just try to tough it out on my own? The answer consistently seemed to be to talk with Wayne.

I could have gone to another mentor to our group for counsel, but I chose Wayne. It was a decision I questioned much over the years that made me wonder: what did I intuitively see in him that on some deep, unconscious level, made me know things would turn out as they did? This was a critical turning point in my life, and many things opened up as a result of that conversation. Pain, awareness, and freedom came out of it for me, not because of Wayne, but in spite of him. I still believe I was spiritually guided to his office that day, just not for the reason I thought.

Chapter 2

I got out of my car, walked across the parking lot to the glass fronted office building. I walked into the lobby, finding the elevator, somewhat dazed because I was going so far outside my comfort zone. I took the elevator to the second floor, then walked to the doorway of Wayne's office suite. I don't even remember what the office sign listed as the company name, or the type of company. I knew Wayne did something in the oil industry. For a number of years I had bought oil and gas leases all along the Texas Gulf Coast. I had seen Wayne's family name on deeds from Beaumont to south of Corpus Christi. I'd seen Wayne's name on many of those deeds, receiving mineral interests in large tracts from what appeared to be either his father or grandfather. All the transactions were in areas of heavy oil activity.

I knew the oil industry had done well for Wayne—Ivy League education, palatial home in River Oaks—the wealthiest neighborhood in Houston. Wayne had started with a lot of family money and resources and had evidently built upon that. But what he did currently, the office did little to clarify. As I stepped inside the door, it looked similar to numerous independent oil company offices I had visited in the course of work. I gave my name to the receptionist, told her I was here to see Wayne, and took a seat. I was nervous—like I'd normally get before a softball game—jittery. But I was now committed. When I had called Wayne the previous weekend to set up an appointment, I hadn't specified what I wanted to talk about. So it wasn't too late to change my mind and just talk about getting some guidance in a general way. But I knew I had to go through with this—had to be straight about my situation, and ask for his help. The receptionist walked back into the room, smiled and motioned to me, and I got up to follow her. Here we go!

She led me down a short hallway, past a secretary's desk, and then stopped, stood aside, and waved her hand, motioning me through another doorway. Doorway? Was that what you'd call it? It was unlike anything I'd ever seen. There was a frame—an old, faded, weather-beaten wood panel surrounding the door. It was large—probably about 9 feet by 6 feet, planted in the middle of an otherwise ordinary office wall. There was a threshold across the base of the doorway, rising about 4 inches from the ground. You had to step over the threshold to pass through, and it created the effect of stepping through a hatch in an old sailing ship. It was terribly out of place in an office setting, and I'd never seen anything remotely close to it. It distracted me so much that it took a moment to gather myself and smile at Wayne, who was rising from his desk.

Wayne came over, shook my hand, and offered me a seat on a couch next to the window. The receptionist had followed me in and now asked if I'd like something to drink. I told her I'd like a coke, and there was a polite pause while she went to get it. Wayne took a phone call, and it gave me a chance to look around the office. It was a very large room—the size of a typical conference room. He had an enormous, dark wooden desk opposite the odd looking doorway; I believe there was a small conference table toward the interior of the building. The couch where I sat backed a long panel of windows and had expensive leather chairs on either side of it. With all that furniture in the room there was still a lot of open space. The wooden floors had several large area rugs. Mounted on the walls were a number of stuffed trophy animal heads—I believe there was an antelope, possibly a lion's head, and several others. I remembered that Wayne and his wife had gone big game hunting in Africa, and I concluded the animal heads were from that adventure.

It was all pretty gaudy, even for the offices I had visited in the oil companies. Flair wouldn't be quite the right word. Showy—in some way I couldn't decipher in my nervousness about the upcoming discussion. I was uncomfortable with what I saw in Wayne's office, but didn't know why.

And to my right was the doorway. It loomed larger and more conspicuous as I had a moment to study it. It really did look like a hatchway on an old pirate ship. It looked like what you might find if you asked Huck Finn to decorate for you. I couldn't pull my eyes from it. I knew it was telling me something—I just couldn't figure it out right then. But it puzzled me mightily.

As I looked at it, the receptionist stepped over the threshold, walked over and set a cup of ice and a coke on the coffee table in front of me, smiled and left, pulling shut the wooden door.

Wayne hung up the phone, walked over and sat in one of the leather chairs. I was lower than him, sitting there on the couch, and felt odd about it. But, no time for that. He smiled, straightened his tie, and said, "So how's it going, Dan?" I took a sip of coke, took the plunge, and began to speak.

Chapter 3

I thanked him for seeing me, told him I needed some help, and then sketched out the trouble I was having finding work, which condition I believed was short term. I had gotten a short term contract in the oil business that summer, but the oil industry was in a major slump, and it had been tough to find jobs. I had told Wayne I was also feeling some resistance to getting a job which I couldn't figure out. He didn't say anything, but just listened quietly. Then I got to the heart of the real spiritual growth I'd been experiencing, and the wonderful direction that had opened up for me.

"I think I'm going to go back to school and get a creative writing degree. To be able to fully steward my writing gift." I thought Wayne, of all people, would understand the magnitude and power of that direction. Looking beyond the short term problems I was having, this was a way to use my talents at a whole new level. A writing talent in particular, that Wayne himself had supported me in accessing. I looked at him as I said this, and was surprised by the frown on his face. Wayne at one point had suggested I find a writing mentor—that I sit at the feet of a master to study the craft. Now I was telling him I had found a way to do that, and he showed no pleasure, no joy about what I was claiming.

But it was time to get back to the here and now. I told Wayne I'd been having trouble paying my bills, and making my car payment—just temporary, of course, but it was a struggle right now. I gulped and pressed on. I concluded by saying, "So to get me through this time until I can get back on my feet, I'd like to ask for the loan of all or part of $3,000." There, I'd said it—I'd asked for help. Now it was up to Wayne. I sat and waited, watching him intently. Wayne sat quietly for a few moments and I could tell he was gathering his thoughts. Then he spoke. "Dan, you say you need some help to get back on your feet, but it looks more serious than that. You really have your back on the asphalt. Your friends are all concerned about you." I just sat and listened, a sinking feeling developing in my gut.

"You're having trouble making your car payments. If you can't find work, maybe it's time to give up your car and ride the bus." He sat for a moment, then resumed, "You need to find some work—and soon. You've stiffed your creditors." He sat and thought for a moment, then continued. "And what does writing have to do with earning a living? Based on your track record from the past two years, your writing and career plan is just a fantasy. I'd be willing to help you out, but I want to be clear—are you asking for a loan, or a gift? Just so we can be clear on what's going on here. It's a loan if you have a plan—if not, it's just a gift.

"I think the first thing to do is for you to show me you're serious about working again. You need to find some work—and soon," he repeated. "Call me when you've got some work and we'll go from there. You're close— you're so close."

He paused, seeing the stricken look on my face. "Dan, I understand what you're going through. Really I do. I've been where you are, I've felt that place of having no money. I really would like to help you. But I can't unless you help yourself." I nodded my head, not sure what to say. Wayne stood and I automatically stood as well. He shook my hand, walked me across his office to another ordinary door over in a corner, opened it for me and I passed through. I think I gave him a tepid "thank you" for seeing me as I left, and I was back out in the hall outside his office suite. I went back to my car, got in, opened a small notebook I kept there, and began to write what had just happened.

CHAPTER 4

I was mad—really, really angry. As I wrote, I reflected. I wanted to write down the things Wayne had said so I wouldn't forget. His words tumbled out onto paper. *"Your friends are all concerned about you."* Really? I hadn't heard about this. None of them had said anything to me. So I was the topic of conversation—someone had expressed concern about me to Wayne—and was I an object of pity or something? That really rankled me.

"Maybe it's time to give up your car and start taking the bus." On the face of it, that seemed to make some sense, but the way he said it—hard to pin down how—made it feel like he was calling me a failure. It was an affront to my dignity.

The anger was boiling now. I kept writing. *"You've stiffed your creditors."* This really hurt. He made it sound intentional—like I went out of my way to avoid repaying my debts. Anyone who knew me would know I didn't do things like that. He attacked my reputation and that may have cut the deepest.

"What does writing have to do with earning a living?" Now he was trying to crumble my dreams—my vision for my life, my spiritual path. For someone who had supposedly been an advocate for my writing, this was a pretty strange statement. He robbed my dream of its beauty.

"Given your track record for the last two years, your writing and career plan is just a fantasy!" It felt like he was saying I was out of touch with reality, that I had my head in the clouds. That statement gave me no credit for clear thinking, for being able to attain a goal. I began to see it—he was trying to take everything from me—that's the way it felt.

Then he had said something that strongly questioned my integrity. *"Is this a loan or a gift?"* That was close to saying he didn't believe I would pay him back. Did he really think I'd do that to someone—and intentionally? First he said I was betraying my creditors, and now he was saying he thought I would betray him. It felt like he was saying I wasn't trustworthy. I was reeling as I was writing all of this down. I looked outside the car to try to regain my balance, my composure. I watched the landscaping crew as they loaded their equipment back on a trailer. Had it been that short a visit with Wayne?

"I've been where you are." This statement just didn't make sense. When was he down and out like I was now? I'd seen the recorded deeds, the amount of land he had inherited from his family. It violated reason to think he had ever actually experienced being broke.

"You're really close." Close to what, close to where? To some spiritual place he thought I should be? Was that what the whole exercise was about—him trying to orchestrate some kind of surrender experience for me? I had told him about the changes I'd gone through over the summer, letting go of my will for how things had to be. But he had disregarded those experiences. Could it be he wanted credit if I had some kind of spiritual breakthrough? *"You need to get some work right now."* That statement certainly did make sense—but it was delivered with a sort of condescending tone—like he really didn't think I would find work. After all, in his opinion I was living in a fantasy world. I had tried to tell him that I felt some really deep resistance to getting a job, but he disregarded that statement also. Later I would understand the job issue in a whole new light, but for the moment, I just felt like I was being challenged, but in a taunting way, not in a supportive way.

That really was the essence of it. Seeing the transcript of the conversation, an outside observer would think Wayne was making valid points. But the way his comments came across—it felt like a schoolyard bully kicking a man when he was down. There were undercurrents going on that felt like they didn't have anything to do with me. Did he put down my writing dream because he, himself, was a frustrated writer? There was a subtle, sarcastic, sneering tone to his speaking that wouldn't come through when reading the written text of the conversation. But it was there—I heard it. It felt like the old stunt where the coach intentionally tries to make the player mad so he'll try harder. But in this case, badly misapplied. I felt violated. Ripped apart—my dignity, my reputation, my dreams, all shredded. If he thought this was some sort of tough love exercise on his part, he didn't deliver it that way. It felt like it was just intended to hurt, to put down, to shame. And I was mad about it. As I started my car, I had to take several deep breaths to regain control before pulling out of the parking lot. I drove off thoroughly angered and disappointed. The doubts didn't begin to seep in until later.

Chapter 5

That year I was living in a garage apartment in a neighborhood called West University, so called because it was west of the Rice University campus. My apartment was behind a two-story house, and located in back of a three-car garage. It had always felt very safe to me, tucked away out of sight, quiet and private. I had a garage stall that faced a door into my apartment. Usually I relaxed when I pulled up the driveway and into the garage. Today was different though. I had a doubt quietly nagging at me—at the back of my mind, almost out of sight, but where it bothered me nonetheless. My landlady was a distant relative of one of my friends—one of the friends Wayne had said were so concerned about me. Now I wondered if my friend had been getting information about me from my landlady. I didn't feel quite as safe as I walked into my apartment. The landlady could readily observe my comings and goings—her kitchen sink faced the garage, and she could see the door in the garage that led to my apartment as she washed dishes. She was a sweet old lady, and could possibly give away information about me without realizing there was any harm in it. I knew some of these friends had been alarmed at some of my activities the last several years. First, I wasn't on the career fast track. A number of my friends were invested in prestigious jobs, but my heart wasn't in pursuing that path, so I hadn't done so, and I know that puzzled some people. No, that wasn't really accurate. I had wanted to climb a career ladder toward a prestigious job. But the path eluded me. I would set out toward a job direction, only to see it fizzle out—to the point I had begun to feel cursed in some way—doomed to a life of mediocre jobs, and not sure why. Which only increased my frustration at seeing my friends freely seeking and accepting career advancement.

Also, I had gone outside the church for some of my support. I had been actively involved at St. Luke's Methodist Church for a number of years, and had a lot of friends through that connection. While I was still fairly involved at the church, I had also found a 12 Step group called Adult Children of Alcoholics that met a lot of needs for me. In that group I found people who understood and also struggled with many of the same problems I'd been trying to overcome for years: low self-esteem, trust and relationship problems, isolation, being too dependent on other people. I'd tried over the years to express what was going on for me, but my church friends didn't seem to understand, while the people within ACA understood. In fact, a basis for the group was a common set of characteristics that described me very accurately—and helped crystallize things that for years had been vaguely defined, yet which I felt bogged me down and in some way controlled me.

I know my involvement with that group puzzled some of my long-time friends. One of those friends even went with me to an ACA meeting one time, but acted very nervous and left part way through the meeting. For several years, I'd had the feeling I might not be the only one of our group who was struggling with those issues, but it was never addressed. Only later did I realize—and have confirmed by several in the group—that most of our group had the issues addressed within the ACA program but were unwilling to address them.

So on some level, I knew I wouldn't find support from that group of friends, and as well, was not surprised that they were expressing concerns about me. I was very uneasy that they were talking to Wayne about me, and not talking to me directly. Yet some of the things Wayne had said to me began to work on me as I sat in my apartment, and I began to wonder. I had written in my journal several months before that I was either on a faith journey, going where I felt God wanted me to go, facing old demons to be released of them—or I was going crazy. There didn't seem to be any middle ground. And now that set of choices resurfaced.

Was Wayne seeing it right—was I *"in a fantasy, unwilling to face the harsh realities of life?"* It was another thing he had said that I just remembered as I sat there. Or was I right—intuitively led to struggle with issues that seemed defined and clarified by the experiences I was now involved with? If Wayne was right—then God had deceived me about the path I was on. That's how it felt. God had let me down and I had been following what I thought was His will—which had been a false lead. Which touched the nerve of my deepest fear—instead of being on a walk of faith, being freed by God to pursue a life of happiness, I had been deluded—I was in some way incapable of grasping the realities of life, and was feeble-minded and ill-equipped to make a go of it.

I could feel my mind beginning to spin and bubble, and thoughts appeared that spiraled me downward. I felt myself powerless to stop the thoughts. Some part of me could tell that I had really been mind robbed by Wayne and had a barrel of anger still left, but the ember was quickly dying. My anger at Wayne had begun to turn inward and disappear, shifting to self doubt and a depressed feeling, as I began to believe he was right. What if all the money and job struggles I'd been through were not about working out trust issues— learning to trust God? What if instead it had been a creation of my self-will—to avoid a working world for which I was ill suited? If that was so, then all the growth and sense of freedom I had felt might have been illusory as well. Then I was just the misguided, pitiful slob who just couldn't adjust, doomed to a life as an object of pity by those who could adjust.

I had decided in August, after going through a very low period, that life was a choice. I had given up hope, despaired of ever feeling happy; I'd had thoughts of ending it all, to spare myself the lifetime of a painful future that was all I could envision. I went into a deep valley, and though I prayed to God, it felt like He was not listening. The feelings broke and seemed to diminish, and I thought at that point I had released old feelings about choosing not to live. I thought I had felt Wayne's love toward me in how he was treating me—but was it a loving act misapplied, or a cruel act that eroded my reality to a pitiful, questioning state? I couldn't tell. But this was the closest I had come to feeling hopelessly depressed since that night in Madisonville eight years ago. It was not hard to go back to that night—I felt in such a similar place.

Chapter 6

In October 1979, I had been sitting in a motel room in Madisonville, Texas, feeling suicidal. It seemed like something that had been building for a long time. And it continued to revolve around jobs. Why?

I think I first noticed something when I was about 20 years old. Along with several of my friends, I had been working through the summers on a maintenance crew for a group of food stores in the Fort Worth area. By the time we were about halfway through college, my friends had moved on to other jobs—jobs more suited to being halfway through college—engineering internships, summer help at an oil company. I was still working on the maintenance crew for minimum wage, frustrated and angry. I didn't look for a better job—in fact, the thought never occurred to me. I didn't know why—I never really questioned it seriously.

In my senior year of college, I decided to get a graduate degree. I was honest enough with myself that I could admit that I went to graduate school to postpone the process of getting a real job. So I went to graduate school in business. But even that was a struggle. I went on scholastic probation, which didn't make any sense. I had made good grades all through college, and now it was like I was hitting a wall. After a year in school, my money had run out, and I went to Oklahoma, lived with my parents, and worked in the oilfield. I didn't even tell the crew I had been in college—to avoid being teased as the "college boy." Yet my frustration grew—I knew I was working at jobs that were below my potential, felt like I was stuck in a less than place, but I also felt helpless to break out of it; I felt trapped in that mind set—and had no idea why.

When I went back to finish graduate school, money was still short, and I took a part-time job—changing tires at a tire store. It began to feel humiliating that I kept ending up in low paying jobs. On some level I resisted finishing school and even had to ask the father of a friend for financial help—but I finished.

I interviewed some my last semester, and could tell I was freezing up in the interview process, and got no job offers. The same friend's father pulled some strings, and I got an offer from a major oil company. I went to work in their administrative department, at a bachelor degree entry-level position, after having just received a Master's Degree in Business Administration. My puzzlement grew, along with the frustration of doing work that used less than my potential. It was work that was easy for me, but without much challenge, and I chafed at doing it.

I applied for a job in the land department at the company, where people worked with oil and gas leases and the development of producing properties. I had studied oil and gas law in graduate school, thoroughly enjoyed the course, and really wanted to do that type of work. Since I had applied for a transfer out of the administrative department, I believe the manager took that as an insult. I was re-assigned to tedious, boring duties; I believe in an attempt to make me quit the company.

The transfer to the land department didn't come through and I began interviewing with another oil company for the same position in the land department. I went to Dallas to interview and felt myself freeze up and become very passive during the interview and during lunch with the land manager. I felt it happening but couldn't break out of it.

I was so thoroughly dissatisfied with my current job that I went ahead and quit. I was counting on the job in Dallas to come through, even though part of me felt uneasy—on some level I knew I might not get the job. I didn't. I wondered how it all fell apart, when initially the prospect had looked so bright. It was clear enough by this point that something was going on—that jobs went wrong for me or didn't materialize, through a dynamic I could not fathom.

A friend connected me with a field landman—someone who worked on contract for the oil companies, going out to oil and gas areas to buy leases for the right to drill wells.

I had a lot of school knowledge about leasing and I had grown up in the oil fields. But I had no experience and was hired for the lowest daily rate currently paid. I was sent to Madisonville, a small town two hours north of Houston. I discovered I had a real flair for the work, and there were aspects of the job that were extremely enjoyable and satisfying, but this was the equivalent of being a field hand—a far cry from the office landman I had aspired to be. My despair over another missed opportunity peaked one night as I sat in the hotel room.

I was still drinking in those days, and had bought a pint of some kind of hard liquor after dinner. I always had alarm bells when I drank—my parents were alcoholics, although they had both been sober and in recovery for a long time. I'd already had a number of incidents of drinking to excess, knew I had the genetic predisposition working against me, and so was leery of what I was doing. But that night I just didn't care, which was the biggest alarm signal of all—I just didn't care. As I sat in the room by myself, I could picture living out my life in frustration—drifting job to job, unhappy in each because I would continually be aware I was capable of better; that I was not using my talents. That part of the despair had a focus—I could see why I'd be giving up hope over jobs—there was a realistic expectation of more of the same pattern.

But the other part of the despair didn't seem to have an origin. As I sat there, I felt myself on the edge of a deep, dark lake—an inky blackness. I could just release, relax and let myself fall into that oblivion. I could feel it. My heart hurt with the dark blackness of it. I began to feel it would have been better that I had not been born. I was a burden to my friends, a gypsy who couldn't find a place. I didn't seem to fit anywhere. I didn't contribute anything to the world. No one seemed to understand this black void I faced. I'd tried to talk about it to a friend once or twice, with little success. Life was pain. I began to see that life had been more about pain for many, many years than I had realized. I wasn't feeling anything new—the old black void had just surfaced to the point where I could sense it, feel it, taste it. It was like a leaden weight pulling my heart through the floor.

I began to think it would be easier if I just took charge and killed myself. At least that way, I could shorten the time I'd have to feel that unbearable weight of pain I had uncovered. In my imagination, I could feel the gun in my hand, feel it going up to my head. For some reason, it would have to be a gun. The image was so strong it scared me deeply. I knew I had to connect with someone—right then. I called the woman I was dating—it was unfair to call her in that state, I somehow knew. But I was drowning and needed a life ring. I talked with her awhile. I didn't mention the suicidal thoughts directly—I don't think. I was scared to say it out loud—those types of thoughts meant you were crazy, and I didn't want that label.

But whether I said it directly or not, she got it—she knew I was in a deep, dark place. The next day, upon my return to Houston, two of my friends showed up at my door to take me to dinner. I was puzzled by their sudden appearance. I found out several years later the woman had called them because she was afraid I was going to kill myself. Hmm. Those were some of the friends that Wayne must have referred to as being "concerned about me." So there would have been a focal point for my friends being worried about me. I would have to agree, with my previous history, such concerns about my mental well-being would be valid.

But that valley had taken place eight years ago. I hadn't felt that way since then—or had I? I knew I'd had an underlying sense of unhappiness—but I didn't think it still ran that deep. Yet—undeniably, now I was in a place that felt just like that night in Madisonville, only more real, more tangible. Part of me was puzzled—why would the things Wayne said to me bring up such a deep and visceral reaction? It seemed wildly out of proportion. Why was this coming up, why was this coming up now, and where was this coming from? For right now, I just knew I was on the edge.

Chapter 7

After my talk with Wayne, most of my long-time friends being "concerned about me" made me leery of going to them for support. In my mind, the crazy label was hanging out there, and I didn't want it stuck on me. I wasn't sure where I had gotten the message; I just knew I never wanted to fall into the category of being called crazy. Bad things could happen to you if you were called that. So I needed someone I could trust. The previous summer, I'd been in a men's grief therapy group. Aha! I trusted Belinda, the therapist who had worked with us. She had insight into my issues from our therapy work. On Saturday afternoon I called her, and made arrangements to meet her that evening for coffee at Dobie's café out on North Gessner Road.

I needed the reassurance of having some human contact soon. I could tell the suicidal thoughts were becoming much more real than the night in Madisonville. I had even visualized how it would happen. It would still be with a gun. Fortunately, there were no guns in my apartment. It was curious how that had happened. When I was 14 my Dad had bought me a hunting rifle—a Winchester .30-.30. I was very proud of owning that gun—it admitted me, through some mysterious mechanism, to the fraternity of men. The year after my Dad bought the rifle for me I got to go hunting with my Dad, several of his friends, and their sons, in northwest New Mexico. It was a frightening experience for me, sitting in the back of a pickup on a snowy, grey day, with the other sons. The Dads sat in the warm cab, passing around a whiskey bottle, driving down oil field roads looking for deer. I felt miserable and completely unsafe. The experience had killed my appetite for hunting, and the previous summer I had realized that I hadn't hunted in 20 years, had no desire for it, and I had sold the rifle.

Also in the house had been a .38 revolver, bought seven years before, for home protection or some such justification. I got a pistol mostly because several of my friends had guns, and it was somewhat of a novelty. But for some reason about three weeks earlier, I had decided to sell that pistol. Just as I didn't really have a good reason to buy the pistol, I didn't really have a good reason to sell it. But I had nonetheless.

Yet now, on Saturday afternoon, sitting in my apartment, somewhere deep in my soul, I was wildly glad those guns were gone. Part of me knew if there had been guns in the house I might not survive Saturday night. *Gun—Dan—death* were all trapped in my brain by some thread I couldn't pin down, but it was a powerful connection. The most disturbing thought about it was that in some way, it felt like my destiny to die by a gun—and that somehow I deserved it. I had no idea where that thought came from. But I was sweating at how real it felt, and sat through the afternoon in a quiet terror at what I was feeling. I couldn't wait to see someone who felt safe, who might help me get through this place, to help me regain some balance.

Later I sat in the cafe, across from Belinda, looking at the horrified expression on her face. I had just told her the things Wayne had said to me, and a bit about the suicidal thoughts since.

"So he really did a number on you," she said, "didn't he?"

I nodded.

"He robbed your dignity."

A nod.

"He robbed your reputation."

A nod.

"He robbed your creativity."

Another nod. I just looked at her, tired of thinking about it all.

"And this guy is supposed to be a Christian?"

I raised my palms in puzzlement.

"Sounds more like a schoolyard bully to me." She sat and thought for a minute. "And you've had thoughts of killing yourself?"

"Yes."

"Dan, something's not adding up. The things this jerk said to you were pretty awful—no way around it. But there's something else involved, something deeper, not about today."

I felt relieved—a deep sense of relief—she understood. I gathered my thoughts. "Thanks for saying that, Belinda. I was thinking the same thing. Something's out of whack."

"It sure is. OK—don't think, just tell me the first thing that comes to mind. Finish this sentence: I should kill myself because..."

"I deserve to die."

"Why?"

"Because I'm a bad son."

"Son?"

I sat for a moment—I hadn't realized I'd said that. "So you think this is about my Dad?"

"It sure sounds like it. Tell me this—have you pictured how you would do it—do you have a plan?"

"Yes. I could see it, and the only way I picture it is with a gun, sitting in my living room late at night."

"What kind of a gun?"

"Probably a rifle."

"Complete this sentence then. I should be dead because..."

"My Dad wants me dead." My eyes widened as I realized what I had just said. Belinda looked amazed. She said, "Why does your Dad want you dead?"

"Because hates me. He hates himself."

"Which is it?"

"I couldn't tell you—I don't know. I don't even know where that thought came from."

Belinda frowned, thought for a few moments. I sat quietly and watched her. I felt nothing, had nothing left to offer. I didn't know where to go with all of this. I was numb, and deathly tired.

Belinda bit her lower lip, looked at me. "OK—where all this is coming from is not the point right now. It's about your Dad—that's pretty evident. The thing now is not to act on it. Are you good at keeping your word?"

I misunderstood her. "What, are you talking about when Wayne asked if he was giving me a gift or a loan? Do you mean, would I have paid him back? Of course I would."

She was shaking her head. "No, not that. If you make a promise to me, will you keep it?"

"Oh," I said, beginning to see. "Yes, I'm very good about that. If I tell you I'm going to do something, I do it. If I don't think I can do it, I won't commit to it."

"Good. Would you be willing to commit to me that if these suicidal thoughts come up again, and you think about killing yourself, you'll call somebody, and get some help until the thoughts pass?"

I could have hugged her right then, I was so relieved, but I just sat there quietly and nodded. "Yes, I can do that. I commit to you that if I think about killing myself, I will get some help right away." I knew how I was about things like that. With the insurance of that promise, I could make it. Belinda and I talked for a few more minutes, and then I went home. I knew from her responses that she could tell how close I had been—the alarm never left her face until my commitment to her. Yet I somehow knew if I could get through Saturday night, I'd be alright. For some reason demons like this came up the most on Saturday nights. I wondered what that was about.

I drove home, read a book for a while. I was tense inside, wondering if the thoughts would come, and if they did, how strong they would be. Thank God all the guns were gone! Finally, about two a.m, I drifted off to sleep. I woke up the next morning feeling spent and depleted—like I'd run a long race the day before. In a sense I had; and I had won—for the moment. I could tell that whatever deep inside me had brought up the whole suicidal episode wasn't gone—but I seemed detached from it in a way. I didn't know why I knew this—but on some deep intuitive level I knew it was not about me—about who I was as a human being. It had to do with my Dad—how that was I couldn't say. But it gave me enough edge to climb out of that pit and begin to let go of that place. And there was a glimmer of anger beginning to show through. Damn it—Wayne robbed me! But evidently my dad robbed me even more. I was going to sort this out. I didn't want it to end the way it almost had on Saturday.

Chapter 8

Perspective began to return on Monday. I talked to Karen, a friend from church who had been to classes where Wayne had taught. She knew him, knew me and much about my struggles, and was deeply intuitive. I trusted her viewpoint a lot. I told her what had happened with Wayne, being as objective as I could about what had been said.

"Dan, Wayne has a big ego. He was fine with you as long as he could be the mentor and you were his follower. But I think he's been mad at you since you started going out on your own path; since you stopped being his helper at the prison ministries and going to his Bible studies."

"So you don't think what he was saying was accurate? About what I've been struggling with?"

"Accurate? Dan, it's an outright misrepresentation. Look at how he has you doubting. You're on a walk of faith and he's not."

"He's not?" I was shocked. Wayne was widely regarded as a great spiritual leader.

"Dan, Wayne is all tied up in what people do. He's very swayed by status and prestige. He's stuck in his head. He knows it all intellectually, but not emotionally. And he was being inconsistent. He was focusing on your circumstances, and not looking at your faith—while walking by faith was part of what he taught."

"So all that talk about how he's been where I am?"

Karen scoffed at that and didn't even bother to reply. I felt better after that, because Karen had put words on what my intuition had been telling me, and had confirmed what Belinda had been telling me.

That night I prayed and told God I felt alive again. He had raised someone from the dead—me. From the spiritual death of trying to live up to false gods, and the physical wish for death I was beginning to suspect I had carried since I was a teenager. I hadn't seen it or actually known about it consciously, but that deep feeling of knowing I was supposed to die had been there for a long, long time. I felt somehow that feeling had been lifted for now—though I still didn't know where it came from.

Since I had gotten into self-doubt, I hadn't been able to feel my anger toward Wayne, but it had definitely been there when I left his office, and I suspected it might resurface eventually. But one thing he had said made sense—I needed to find some work. That was a true statement, and I felt it would help anchor me, give me back a sense of myself. I still had some powerful resistance around looking for "career" jobs, and knew I'd only frustrate myself if I tried to go down that road at the present time. First, because those jobs typically took longer in the hiring process. Second, because job search had been such a painful, frustrating and unsuccessful pursuit. I didn't think I could stand having job possibilities fall through on me right then.

I knew a guy from ACA named Timothy who did house repairs and I thought he might need some help. He did, and when I asked him, he needed someone for the next day. So I went to work—scraping paint, painting, caulking—whatever he needed each day. It felt good to be doing something to have a structure to my day. And this kind of work didn't bring up the anxiety I felt around more career-oriented jobs.

By the end of the week I thought maybe I had overreacted about what had happened with Wayne. So I decided to see if he really would help me. He had said he would be there for me if I got work.

So I called and told him I'd gotten some work. Then I listened—cautiously.

"That's great, Dan. I'll be glad to help you out. Just do this. Bring all your bills, and some written estimate of your monthly expenses, and I'll help you set up a monthly budget and a plan."

I frowned to myself and quick as a heartbeat knew I couldn't do that. I couldn't take the chance that he might put me down again, suck out my soul and make me out to be a deadbeat. Somehow I just knew he didn't want to help—he wanted control—of my soul. I could not let myself get close enough to risk him pulling the life out of me again—I didn't trust him.

"Wayne, no thanks. I believe I'll pass. I think I need to go to someone who has some trust in me."

"OK, Dan, you do what you need to."

He sounded almost angry at my declining his offer. But I knew I'd done the right thing. And at that moment I felt something die. Wayne, one of my heroes—or someone I had thought of as a hero—had fallen. Or maybe it was some need of mine to have a hero. Either way, I felt the loss.

CHAPTER 9

I was puzzled by the feelings of foreboding I'd been having, not seeming to be connected to anything. Particularly, how did I become suicidal over the meeting with Wayne? What was that all about? The experience felt familiar—like an old memory trying to surface. It was a familiar feeling—it had happened several times fairly recently, when I had experienced several buried memories returning to my awareness. Was that what was happening—was I trying to remember something?

The first time it had happened had been a year ago—October of 1986. I really believe it was triggered by a job interview. I had, yet again, been struggling to find my niche in the job world, and had met with the head of an advertising agency about providing copy for ad campaigns. I met with Gerald on a Friday and as usual, the interview process went well. I typically did the interview part well—it was later in the process where it usually seemed to unravel. He told me I had strong educational credentials—a Bachelors' in Marketing and an MBA, as well as presenting myself as very personable, creative—

as someone with good ideas. He gave me a sample task to perform. He told me about an ad campaign they had coming up, and suggested I develop for him a theme and slogan appropriate to the task and present my idea to him on Tuesday.

I agreed and left his office, excited at the possibility. It seemed like a direction that had a strong potential for me, and I wanted to perform well. I had the weekend to come up with an idea, which I did—the juices flowed, the idea coalesced, and I felt ready. Then excitement was replaced by fear. I went to an ACA meeting on Monday, and talked about the experience, and felt the fear rise. Tomorrow I was going to present my creative idea, and place a value on it. Just thinking about it made me begin to quiver, and I shook with fear as I had never done before. My whole body shook as I lay in bed at home, unable to move. At the time, I was involved in a group that showed how to process and release old, stuck feelings. For me, fear released by shaking, like someone would do after a car accident or a scary event. I had learned to just go along and not fight the shaking, because it really did release old fears—it had begun to work for me, and I would feel lighter and more free after it had happened.

The tremors began to ebb, and suddenly I could tell it had something to do with my Dad and my 8th grade literary magazine, and the fact that my Dad never talked much. I somehow feared success—I feared the ad agency man liking my work. I felt some deep block—I could not remember; but there was something there.

In 1964 our family was living in Farmington, a small town in northwest New Mexico. Our 8th grade English class had decided to publish a literary magazine for our school. It was an exciting project which kept us involved through the winter and into early spring. We thrived on the creative process—we were free to submit our work to the magazine. Our class had begun writing short stories, we had dabbled in various poetry forms—and I thoroughly loved the process. I had one short story and five poems published, and I was terribly excited about it. Yet shortly after that, I was not writing at all—writing had no joy in it—I could barely finish term papers in college, struggled intensely to finish my master's thesis, and writing was no longer a pleasure. Something had taken place—a shift as sudden as turning off a light. What had happened? It was like looking into a darkened room to try and remember—but I could almost sense more than see, a glimmer of light and comprehension far back in the darkness. Somehow my Dad squashed my creativity—did he say something?

Tuesday I met with Gerald and it only heightened the sensation of being in a place I had been before. I had come up with a terrific idea for an ad campaign—it was brilliant, I knew it and I could feel it. Yet it brought up more fear than excitement as I waited to meet with him. I walked into his office; he was distracted and began talking about separating from his wife. I was not there to listen to that, so I gently guided the conversation back to my work—pulled us back to business. I showed him my idea, and he didn't say much—it almost seemed like he was not even paying attention. He just looked at it and said he'd talk it over with his staff. I was disappointed by his tepid response.

I had contemplated a lot about what to charge him for my work. Gerald had said $30 an hour was the top rate for a copy writer, and I had decided to be bold—to charge him $60, which would be $30 an hour for two hours of work—to value myself fairly, but send a signal that my time was valuable, that my work was valuable. He sat there still looking distracted, and I began to feel he wasn't even going to ask how much this idea would cost, should he choose to accept it. I volunteered my price and he seemed almost indifferent to it, but didn't object to my rate. I left his office feeling deflated and discouraged. I could tell he wasn't going to use my idea—but somehow felt it wasn't that it was a bad idea—just not what he was looking for. Either that, or his head just wasn't in the game right then. Regardless—it only compounded the feeling that I was looking into the dark room of my memories. This stirred up something. I just couldn't tell how or what.

I came home, laid down and shook with fear for over an hour. Whatever was trying to come out felt big, deep and old. The same thing—deep shaking with fear—happened several times over the next two days. In between times I would sit and think about junior high. I still had my 9th grade annual—it had pictures of all the same people I'd worked with to create the literary magazine. I would look at the pictures for a long time, trying to put myself back in that time—trying to remember. I still had the literary magazine—"Scholarly Scribbles, 1964." Hermosa Junior High School in Farmington, New Mexico. I had published poems in that magazine, and it was one of the proudest moments in my life. And then it wasn't. I suddenly remembered something. Several months before, someone had heard me speaking in a group, and had asked me afterward if I was a poet. "You have a very lyrical, poetic way of speaking," she had said.

"No, I'm not a poet," I had replied, very emphatically. And at that moment such was my truth. I had blocked out the fact that I had even written poetry, and acted like I wasn't and had never been a poet—and had felt that. It was a strong reaction—almost a panicky, push it away feeling. "No, I'm not a poet!" It was like I couldn't wait to divorce myself from that label. Yet here I was, looking at tangible evidence that I was, indeed, a poet. It was a strong urge, to make me push away part of my being so forcefully. What the hell had happened?

DAN L. HAYS

As I looked through the literary magazine, I was drawn to one of the poems written
by me at age 14, entitled "The Demon". It
began:

A fiery, bubbling demon against the
sky
The huge volcano,
Lava pouring from its lip,
Like angry words hastily spoken.
It seems to be making fun of some-
one below it,
Or trying to shame a person
For doing a wrong.

As I read it, I felt the poem was about my
Dad. I could just tell it from the words. But
my Dad never said things—did he? I remembered him being silent when he was angry
with someone. Had he said something? It felt
right—but what had he said? For several
days, I reeled with alternative episodes of
shaking with deep fear, then being able to sit
quietly, but nothing more emerged. Friday I
went to the noon ACA meeting at Holy Name
Retreat Center. I needed to feel safe, and
Holy Name was one of my safest places—a
sanctuary in the truest sense of the word. It
was a long, low building in an island of pine
trees in the middle of a quiet residential
neighborhood in west Houston, and driving
onto the grounds, you could feel the release
and unwinding of tension. This was a safe
place, lovely and apart from the world outside.

The meeting room was at the near end of the building, and contained several semi-circles of chairs facing where the chairmen and leader sat. It had a coffee bar off to the left, long rows of windows along two walls, looking out onto tall pines trees. I loved that place. I sat down next to Charlene—a very calm person. She and I had been in the feelings group together, and I had come to feel very safe with her and supported by her in having my feelings.

The meeting chairman was someone I knew—the leader was not. It was a large bearded male and I could feel energy radiating from him—ugly, nasty, angry energy. He was a priest, an alcoholic involved in other 12 step programs, and from the way the chairman introduced him—something of a leader in the recovery community. All I could tell was—he didn't feel safe.

He began talking about parenting yourself and at times spoke loudly and angrily. I felt myself tighten, and held Charlene's hand to feel safe. I shared. I talked about how I felt anger in the room, how I almost shut down and couldn't hear—how it felt like Dad and his anger.

Some time later the angry priest exploded, speaking sharply and angrily—the same way Dad's anger exploded sharply—like a firecracker going off. I think he was talking about—emphasizing—that he wasn't angry. But I couldn't be sure of what he said. At one point, he slammed his fist down on the table next to him. I think he was looking at me when he did it. Charlene could feel me jump, and held on to me tightly—as if to reassure me I was safe. The gesture felt just like something familiar; the whole sequence of events felt like I'd lived through it before—but what was it—what did it stir up in me? The slamming fist—that was the key.

I went and saw "Peggy Sue Got Married" to try to calm down. I always felt safe in a darkened theater—no one could find me or hurt me there.

I came home and returned a phone call from a woman in the ACA program named Julie. She said she was in a shame attack and felt like God was getting ready to reveal something to her which she had always run from. It was a huge gift for me to hear that. I told her I was in exactly the same spot, and affirmed I was going to stay home and stay with the feelings. I lay down on the couch and shook with the fear, after fighting it, saying "no, no." I screamed the high hurt of a young boy.

Then I could see it. It was March of 1964, just before suppertime, and I had just come inside the house from the cold night air. In my hand I held the same literary magazine that now lay on my desk. In my heart—there was true joy. I had known since I was 6 years old I was meant to be a writer. It was my destiny, it was my truth. Now I had my first proof and confirmation—I had published! Poems and a short story—and I knew they were good. Beyond the fact that my teacher had praised them—I just knew

46

the things I had written were good. I walked into the living room, where my dad slouched in his easy chair, a drink on the table beside him, sullenly watching TV. He looked angry—and drunk. But I was too happy to correctly read the signs.

I held up my copy of the Scholarly Scribbles magazine. "Daddy, Daddy, guess what? I'm a writer. Teacher says so. We did this literary magazine and I published a short story and five poems!" And I waited—for his approval—which I always desperately wanted. Waited—for his congratulations—which I seldom heard. Waited—for his love—which I was unsure existed.

He looked at me for a long moment. Then he slammed his fist angrily on the arm of his chair and shouted, "Poems! You little shit, you'll never amount to anything!" He looked back toward the TV, as I stood, rooted to the spot totally numb. Somehow I went back to my room, the life sucked out of me. After that I stopped writing, and life wasn't as much fun.

———————

Now, back in my apartment, I shook my head and I came back to reality—as if I had, in the remembering, relived the whole experience. I was exhausted, somewhat numb, but I felt more free and more relaxed having remembered. Intuitively I knew it would take a long time to really appreciate the magnitude of what I had just remembered—how deeply it affected me, and how much release there could be from at last knowing about that moment in time when part of me—I knew this now—had died. As if in confirmation of all of that, a new poem sprang out of my soul the next day—the first I had written since I was fourteen. It was entitled "Heartbeat" and began like this:

> My heart stopped beating
> When I was fourteen,
> Avoiding the pain
> That could rarely be seen.
>
> It hurt me so deeply,
> I pushed it away.
> Never to feel what
> Had happened that day.
>
> I published five poems,
> And bubbling with joy,
> I showed them to Daddy,
> Be proud of this boy.
>
> "You're good for nothing,"
> Dad drunkenly cried.
> In shame I stopped breathing,
> My heartbeat had died.

I was now 36, and a very essential part of me had been dead since I was fourteen. I had died that day—my spirit killed. Yet the poem I had just written was proof that the dead part of my soul could be reawakened; I just sat quietly with that awareness for a long, long time.

Chapter 10

The second time I had a memory crawl back to the surface was several months later, early in 1987, and I was a little more attuned to what was happening as awareness began to bubble up. It was a long process of several things happening that triggered the fear, re-stimulated what had happened when I was a teenager, and brought the memory back to the surface where I could see it.

After I remembered what had happened with the literary magazine, I had begun writing poetry again. It seemed like every two or three days I was writing a new poem—as if all the creativity that had been bottled up for so many years was pouring out of me all at once.

I had mentioned writing poetry again to my Mom, who had asked to see some of what I had written. I agreed, and sent her several of my poems. I didn't send "Heartbeat," because I felt it would be cruel to tell my Dad of that incident via a poem. I felt it was likely he had been blacked out drunk when it had happened and had no memory of the incident. After that time, when I was about 17, my parents had both joined Alcoholics Anonymous, and had been very active and continuously sober for 20 years. His participation in that program had led to a lot of healing between my Dad and I.

My parents came to Texas for my sister Kitty's wedding in February of 1987, and I met the family in Austin. When I saw my parents at the motel, my Mom said she liked my poetry, and then my Dad later said he liked my poetry also. It seemed like an innocent compliment at the time, but I realized much later it brought up a lot of old feelings—mostly fear—because hearing my Dad praise my poetry was such a contradiction to his statement over the literary magazine. I was edgy the rest of the weekend—throughout the wedding process—and I think it was due to that moment in the hotel lobby. It threw me into an old place completely apart from the wedding I was attending. I even had to leave the reception for a while and go off by myself, to get away and try to calm down.

After the wedding, I left the next day, earlier than I had intended, because I felt so fearful and uneasy. I was drained from the rush of the wedding, but there was something else going on I couldn't quite pin down. I didn't feel safe—it was the first time I had been around my parents in a year. Things were more comfortable with my Dad than I ever remembered them being—yet I didn't feel safe. Back in Houston, I was surprised that the fearful feelings persisted, but at least I could be in my comfort space—have a quiet place to be at home, talk to friends, go to meetings, and try to get in touch with where this fear was coming from.

By Monday, I was in a massive amount of fear—fear not connected to any thing in the present. I lay in bed frozen. It felt like I physically could not move. It was a paralysis of fear which had immobilized me before. I had planned that morning to go over to the Rice University Library to begin exploring writing as a career, and how to get an education as a writer. And now I couldn't move.

I prayed to God to release me from the fear, because I was utterly powerless. I felt so incapable of taking the next step of faith, claiming my writing, my talents, becoming visible to the world, being happy and enthusiastic. I knew in some way confronting this fear would happen—needed to happen. There was something stuck inside me eating away that needed to be released. Yet I couldn't even surrender to the pain. I was willing, but powerless. I lay in bed and finally shook out a lot of fear. It subsided after a while, and I was able to function again.

Several days later I was able to return to the library. I found out about an NYU publishing workshop in the summer. I found a national poetry competition. I called New York and found out I had just missed the deadline. I had more fear come up, wasn't as surprised this time, and went home, lay on the bed and shook with fear until it finally subsided.

The next day I began formulating a business plan for how to pursue my writing in an orderly way. I formulated a mission statement: "to fully steward my God-given talents in a God-directed yet goal oriented manner." As soon as I wrote that the fear came up again, but not as severely, or for as long. I sensed I needed a break, and stopped work on the writing for a couple of days.

At the same time, I had agreed to do several speaking engagements. The next week I was going to read my poetry to a recovery group gathering, and the first weekend in March I was to speak to a Sunday school class at my church on the topic of surrender. I hadn't connected any of the fear I was feeling to those events, but I would soon come to see that those speaking opportunities were directly stimulating and connected to the fear I was feeling.

The next day something else came up. I felt numb, an odd sensation of darkness. I didn't want to be around people, or go to a meeting where people would want to hug me, or even touch me. I suddenly didn't want to be touched. I sat with the feeling until it subsided, and then went to the gym to work out. I strained a muscle in my back, and my back and neck were stiff like I had a crick. Again, these sensations weren't connected to anything, but I felt somehow they were—almost like a familiar place I had been once before, to which I was returning.

Several days passed, and I was able to go to a meeting again, and be around people.

After the meeting, a woman mentioned about feelings of submerged abuse surfacing. It resonated with me, somehow felt true for me yet I couldn't tell in what way. I was thoroughly mystified as to what was happening to me, yet somehow knew I needed to let things continue to play out.

The next night I lay in bed and shook with fear—I was crying and screaming out loud, and my neck was bowed and tense, like I had felt in the gym. I began to sense that it had something to do with my Dad hitting me, but couldn't tell any more than that.

Two days later, a Thursday, I was supposed to read my poetry for the recovery group. I was shivering with fear all afternoon, yet by the time I arrived at the woman's house where the group was meeting, I had calmed. I read and did it beautifully. I felt the power of the words I had written. One poem in particular got a lot of praise. It was about me, but I guess people related to it. It began:

> My friends have all loved me,
> Through the years did express,
> Their love and their sharing,
> But without much success.
>
> I know they were puzzled,
> When they said a kind word,
> That I did not receive it,
> As if I had not heard.
>
> I thought I could hear them,
> Thought I could receive,

But that someone could love me,
I could not believe.

And I see that their loving me,
Fell on deaf ears.
I thought I was worthless,
Because of my fears.

I got a lot of compliments, both on what I had read, and how I had read it. It felt wonderful, and I took in all the love and affirmation offered me. Diane, a good friend in recovery, even asked me to give her copies of several of my poems. I was astounded at this indication of how much the poems had affected her. One compliment in particular, on another aspect of the evening, caught my attention. A woman name Michelle said, "You really are a good public speaker." I stayed with that thought as I drove home that night and pieces started to connect. I had done speech contests in the 9th grade, very actively, and then suddenly stopped. I almost failed a speech class in college because I would freeze up totally when trying to speak to a group. I began to suspect my speaking was shamed or put down in some way, but I couldn't remember how it had happened.

The next day I awoke feeling exultant over the poetry reading and all the support I received, and as soon as I got excited about it massive fear hit me and I was terrified at the thought of speaking in public. I felt frozen, immobilized; and I was supposed to speak to a Sunday school class of about fifty people in two weeks. I thought first about canceling the talk, and then realized I must walk through and work through this fear or it would continue to build on itself.

I went to a meeting that night and a young woman named Eleanor led. She shared about—I used to be proud of what I did, and then I wasn't any more. Another piece connected for me. I was in a speech contest in the 9th grade. I was proud of doing it, but I didn't win. I came in a second, which was really great—but I didn't win. And then I knew—something happened after the 9th grade speech contest. But what?

I came home and wrote about it. As I wrote, there was a storm outside, the wind was blowing noisily. There was a storm inside me as well. Something was beginning to click and come to light about how my public speaking was shamed. The shame was now right on the surface and I knew—I just knew—I was in the position that, with God's help, I could chase that shame from my body—like purging a cancer. I had talked to someone that day and said that part of what I was supposed to do with my life—in addition to the writing—was public speaking. Saying that out loud had given the words real power, and made the concept come alive to me. I somehow knew as I said it, that those words would bring up the resistance to public speaking that I had been feeling, even more intensely. It did. I surrendered my talk to the Sunday school class—ironic by now that it was on the topic of surrender—and knew my part was just to feel whatever was going on right now—feel the fear.

I sat and reflected on the speech contest. In the 9th grade, our English class was involved in a lot of speaking projects—it was Mrs. Kerr's joy to open kids up to public speaking, so we did it a lot. I remember going to Durango, Colorado for a speech contest, performing a reading of "The Secret Life of Walter Mitty," and winning a prize for it.

But the pinnacle was the Optimist's Club speech contest to be held in March of 1965. As I had that thought, I realized it was now the end of February, 1987—coming up on March. Were some of these feelings coming up now because of the time of year? We were to write speeches on "Optimism—Spirit of Youth" and deliver those speeches in front of the local Optimist's Club. It was a big and exciting contest for us, and we spent a lot of time preparing and practicing in class. The top two winners would go to Albuquerque to compete in the state Optimist's Club contest.

We gave the speeches at a local restaurant on a school night—my Mom was there, Dad didn't come. I came in second—Tim Harrington won. I was told afterward that my speech was four seconds too short—if not for that factor, I would have won first place. I never entered another speech contest after that night. When I returned to Farmington years later, I drove by that restaurant on west Main several times, but it was painful to even look at the place, and I could not bring myself to go inside. What happened? Did my

Dad say something, like he had over the literary magazine? Or did he not say anything and I could feel his disappointment? I didn't know, but I could feel that I was about to find out. I already felt—I knew—I was a nothing, a worthless person, after the poetry incident. Was this proof conclusive? Did something else happen to deepen that belief? I sat in my apartment and wondered.

———

The next day was Sunday and I was supposed to talk to the Sunday school class. Saturday night I went over my notes, rehearsing the talk, and knew I was well prepared. I got ready for bed, turned out the lights, and the pain hit. I started crying, sobbing deeply—as I wasn't able to do years ago. I said out loud, "I wasn't good enough. I talked too fast, and I lost. I was so proud of my speech. Daddy was disappointed, I know he was. Please don't hit me any more, Daddy." I didn't know where that last sentence came from, but as the crying subsided, I had had a crystallizing dread that I knew what it meant. It was about him hitting me after the speech contest, and me connecting it to my failure to win. Somehow it was very important—terribly important—that I win. To show him I could amount to something.

I could feel that there was more I would remember, something still blocked that I couldn't get to. I prayed, "Dear God, show me what I can't see." It felt big, and nasty, and shaming. I could see that it began to emerge Thursday night, after I had read my poetry and the woman said I was really a good public speaker. I could hear and absorb her words that night, and I knew that what she said was true—I really was a gifted speaker. But that just kicked off what came up tonight—it shot the old shame to the surface. I finally drifted off to sleep, feeling hardly in a balanced place to be able to speak in public the next day.

———————

I awoke the next morning in a lot of fear, and very nervous. I asked God to carry me through my talk. I again surrendered the speech, on the topic of surrender. I went to the church and made it through the 25 minute talk. I felt like I was stumbling and very hesitant.

Yet afterward, a curious thing happened. Several people came up and used the word "professional" for my delivery. One lady even asked if I did speaking professionally. Numerous people came up and thanked me for my excellent presentation. I was somewhat dumbfounded, partly at the strength of the compliments and affirmations I received. Yet also puzzled by how all this could be happening with what I went through last night, and how hesitant I felt this morning. I had to get some feedback. Karen had been in the audience when I talked—I asked her what she had seen.

"Dan, it looked like you were of God," she said. "You looked more at peace with yourself, more confident and more powerful than I've ever seen you. There was a lot of affirmation from the group. People were listening carefully, nodding and agreeing with what you said."

I went home, sat and thought about the whole thing—particularly Karen's comments. I accepted what she said as true because I trusted her judgment, but it felt totally unlike my experience of being so hesitant and fearful. I could feel the momentum building—something was about to break loose.

———————

The next day, I remembered that after the poetry incident, I was trying even harder to make my Dad proud of me. I was very talented musically, but I had given up piano lessons when I was 10 because my Dad had commented it was sissy. I hadn't excelled in sports, my Dad's specialty; I had tried out for many sports, but while I was athletically talented I was small for my age, and hadn't found a sport that suited me well. I couldn't make him proud through writing—I wasn't writing at all. I got all excited about the Optimist's Club speech contest. My Dad was a salesman—surely he would appreciate a flair for public speaking. I was very proud of my speech, and wanted him to be proud of it. Meanwhile, my parent's drinking was growing worse, and they were fighting a lot. There wasn't much to be excited about at home. School was my safe place, and the joy of English class a central part of my world.

After I came in second in the speech contest, he didn't say anything. My Dad wasn't paying much attention to me then. My Mom came to the speech contest at the restaurant, but my Dad hadn't been there, and that had hurt. I had gotten to present my speech several times to men's groups around town, as the alternate to the winner, and there was still a lot of attention directed toward the speaking, but Dad hadn't been around for any of it. I found out I had been scheduled to go to the state speech contest in Albuquerque with Tim Harrington. As his alternate I would stand in for him should he get sick or something. I came in after school, all excited about my news, desperate to have him be excited for me.

He was in the easy chair, TV on, drink by his side, just as he had been last year when I told him about the literary magazine. I didn't realize the similarity, the potentially negative implications.

"Daddy, guess what! I get to go to Albuquerque. We're going to the state speech contest for the Optimist's Club. If Tim gets sick, I'd have to give my speech, and I might win the state contest. Isn't that great?" And I waited—desperately, I waited.

He looked at me for a long moment, a dark, angry frown on his face. He tried to push himself up out of the chair, fell back, pushed harder and lurched up. I was puzzled—did he want to shake my hand? He still hadn't said anything.

He stood in front of me, and quick as a heartbeat, he hit me. He slapped me hard with his right hand, along the left side of my face. I wasn't prepared for it, wasn't expecting it, didn't see it coming, and it spun me around, and to my hands and knees. I was stunned, shocked, confused. I looked up at him through blurry eyes and heard him say, "I don't want to hear any more about that damned speech."

As if he didn't want to look at me, he turned and picked up his glass, and walked in to the kitchen to fix himself another drink.

Through the numbness, I felt myself push up to my knees and then stand, weaving slightly with dizziness. I didn't want to be there when he came back. I could feel a warm place along the side of my face—like his hand was imprinted there. I felt something running from my nose, put my hand up to it, looked at my hand and there was a small smear of blood.

Like a marionette, I felt myself wobble from the living room into my bedroom. I wanted to be away, to be somewhere else, to be safe, but it was too cold to go outside. I went in my room, closed the door, and felt—nothing. It was like part of me had died. I was proud of what I did, and now I wasn't any more. And he hit me—because I wasn't good enough, because I hadn't won. I deserved to be hit, and Daddy didn't want to know about my life. I sat in the dark for a long time, feeling nothing.

Yet it was not quite nothing. Deep, deep inside, almost where I couldn't touch it, see it or feel it, there was something. Hatred—an ugly hatred. It stayed deep because you're not supposed to hate your Daddy who is supposed to be your idol. But it was there, palpable and pulsating. And with it, a decision: not again—not ever again. I wouldn't let anyone get close enough to hurt me again. Put the walls up high enough, and they won't have a chance—he won't have a chance. I wasn't the same boy who woke up that morning—I never would be again, and somehow I knew that. So I sat in the dark, alone.

CHAPTER 11

In August of 1987 I had remembered a third incident, and it had come to the surface because of therapy work I was doing. I was in a grief therapy group, four men with Belinda as our therapist. We would read painful incidents from our childhood, and typical of ACAs, we would feel very little about what we read. They weren't using the term Post Traumatic Stress Disorder much at this point, but those were the issues we were working on. The benefit of the group was that the other men in the group could access the feelings about what had happened to the reader, and they would give feedback that helped us get in touch with the feelings we had stuffed at the time of the incident. The goal was to release the feelings so we didn't continue to go through life unconsciously ruled by those old incidents. The process was working for me, and had helped me get to and release a lot of old feelings, aided by what I had learned in the feelings group. I had just read an incident to the group about an argument with my Dad about my hair length, a long running point of contention.

My Dad and I had been arguing about my hair for several years. I kept wanting to grow it longer, and he insisted that I keep it burr short, with just a tuft springing up in front—the rest almost bald stubble. But now I was 16, it was 1966, and it was the prime of the Beatles era. A lot of the boys were starting to wear their hair down on their foreheads, loose and shaggy, and I wanted to as well. It was dark outside, a cold winter night. It was dark inside the house as well; few lights were lit, a cavelike atmosphere. It was just after dinnertime and Mom was in the kitchen washing the dishes.

Recently our arguments had taken on an uglier tone; until years later I didn't connect that my Dad had also started drinking more during that time. He was drinking now, had been since he got home from work. I approached him. He was sitting in his easy chair in his familiar position, bourbon and water on the table next to him, a single lamp casting a dim glow, a sitcom chattering at low volume on the TV.

He was in an ugly mood. I should have recognized the warning signs. Or maybe I did, but felt bold or somehow daring, wanting to push his buttons, challenge him. I couldn't understand it myself, why I chose this time to beard the lion.

"Dad?"

"What do you want?"

"Uh, I'm supposed to get a haircut tomorrow, and I want to grow it longer in front, like the Beatles."

"God Damn it, I have told you before, no son of mine is going to grow his hair out like some woman!"

"But Dad, why not? It's my hair. I should be able to wear it like I want to," I said, looking hopefully toward the kitchen, hoping my Mother would come to my aid. I could sense her listening, the noise of dishes in the sink stopping, but no help was forthcoming.

He slammed his fist on the side of the easy chair. It was by now a familiar gesture, but made me jump as always. I stopped breathing, but resolved to keep going with it.

"You will get your hair cut like I tell you to."

"But why; I don't understand," I said, beginning to get angry in spite of the warning signs.

He spoke with a vicious, measured precision, "You will do it because I'm your Father and I say you will!"

"Damn it, Dad, that's not fair. That's not a good enough reason. That's all you ever say is because. Because why? I never get to do anything I want to around here, I mean what's the big deal?" My voice was rising in spite of itself, almost of its own will.

"There is no big deal about it. You will do what I tell you to, you will not argue with me about it, and don't you yell at me!"

"Why not, you're yelling at me?" I could feel myself throwing caution aside, could somehow sense that this was an important point, a time to stand up for myself.

"Damn it, don't you talk to me like that.

This is my house and you will do what I tell you to."

"OK, then, I'll just leave. I'll just pack my bags and run away from home."

"Alright, if that's what you want, I'll help you pack." He stood up, his look dark and ominous, threatening, ugly.

I was so furious I could not speak, but discretion took over and I knew I was about to step over a line from which there was no retreat. I stomped out of the living room, went in to my bedroom, slamming the door.

Once in the bedroom, my heart sank as I realized he had won. I had nowhere to run. I could think of nowhere to go, no one to stay with. I had very little money—he controlled that, so I couldn't take a bus anywhere. We were in a small town in the middle of the desert, and it was winter. There was nowhere to hide.

I sat in the room and brooded. Secretly I harbored a hope that my Mother would come to me, comfort me, and tell me she understood. I wanted to cry, but the tears wouldn't come forth. I paced my bedroom restlessly, feeling trapped, hating him, rageful, frustrated. I couldn't think of anything else to do, so I went to bed.

The therapy group had given me some great feedback on this incident, saying the whole thing felt puzzling, and they could see how I would feel misunderstood, degraded, cheated, unloved, confused, dominated, over-punished, chained, attacked and controlled. I was shocked by how many words they came up with for what I never felt. As they spoke I began to get a glimpse of how I must have felt assaulted back then. The next day I felt the incident even more fully, and I began to get angry about it.

————

My Dad had been in the Marine Corps, so I always wanted to see movies about the Marines to understand more about what made up my Dad. A new Vietnam movie about the Marines had been released that summer called "Full Metal Jacket." I had gone to see it a second time around the time I read about the hair argument in the therapy group. The movie stirred something really deep inside me. It had some scenes about training camp that touched a nerve— one scene in particular—I knew what it felt like. There was one kid in the group, Leonard, who just couldn't get up to speed with the rest of the platoon, and the Drill Instructor used him as a scapegoat to assign extra work to the rest of the group. One night the whole platoon got up late, wrapped towels around him to hold him in his bunk, stuffed a towel in his mouth, then beat him with bars of soap wrapped in towels. The horror and abuse of it had left a deep impression on me. I came home from the movie and lay in bed shaking, feeling terrorized, not knowing what was going to happen next, moaning like Leonard had after he had been beaten. I cried out, "I'm dying." I didn't know where all of this was coming from. I felt self loathing. I had a sick feeling in the pit of my stomach. Daddy hated me. He was beating me—I deserved to die. *Deserved to die? Where did that come from?* Then, as I lay there, I remembered the rest of what had happened the night we argued over my hair. It suddenly came back to me very clearly.

———————

The night we argued about my hair, (I don't know how late it was) I had been asleep for a while when the door of my bedroom swung open violently, banging against the wall. I was startled, half awake, and looked up. The light from the hall framed a silhouette—large, looming, ominous. It was my Dad. I froze; I could not breathe. I couldn't move. What was going on here? I was curled up on my side. I watched as he swayed and lurched toward me. He was breathing deeply, clearly agitated.

He came up beside my bed, an aroma of bourbon flowing before him. Very slowly, he said, "You will not ever talk back to me like that again. Ever, ever, ever."

As he talked he began hitting me with his open hand, along the ribs, hitting, hitting, hitting. I covered up as best I could, curled up in a ball, but he hit me all along my side, my rump, my legs. I was terrified, I went numb, I was in disbelief, shock. I was terrified he would kill me; I didn't know if he would ever stop hitting.

Finally he seemed to wind down; his breath slowed. He stood over me and looked down at me for a long moment, as if mesmerized. He finally turned and left, pulling the door closed behind him.

I lay there shivering for a long time. I couldn't believe it. I felt hated. Why did Daddy hate me? I was ashamed. I felt in some deep mysterious way I must have deserved what he did, but I couldn't understand it. My soul cried out desperately though my voice uttered no words. I felt so alone; I longed for human comfort, but touching meant pain. I was confused.

Underneath it all was a seed which was continuing to germinate, still deeply buried where I could barely sense it, nor consciously acknowledge it to myself. The hatred that I had felt after the speech contest continued to fester. A hatred so deep, so pure, and by now so violent that it frightened me. I longed to be large enough that he could never do that to me again, yet also that I might be able to punish him as he did me. I longed to pound his face into mush, to hit and hit and hit and hurt. Deeply.

But the feeling split me in two. I could not acknowledge the hatred on a conscious level because the other side of me still worshipped him, adored and idolized him, loved him, with all his faults. It made me ashamed of myself for having such thoughts about him. Children should not think that way— honor thy father and mother.

So I was trapped, torn. I still needed his

approval, his love, his tenderness. I had not felt tenderness from him for many years, but the memory of it motivated me to try and recapture that feeling. Yet if I were to get that affection, my hatred would make me reject it. All of this schism was buried so deeply within me I could not express it, even had it been safe to do so.

But I could feel the opposing forces of love and hate struggling within me, and on some level, I knew they were tearing me apart. Something within me was dying.

Chapter 12

I had remembered the poetry incident over the literary magazine in October 1986. The speech incident had returned in March 1987, and I had remembered the argument over my hair in August of 1987. And now I sat in my apartment two months later—October 1987—and thought about it all. I reflected on the magnitude of the suicidal feelings I had experienced, after talking with Wayne, the feeling of something deeply buried within me—was I about to remember something else? Something deeper? Intuitively it made sense—the drinking only got worse in the next two years. In 1964, the poetry incident had happened. In 1965—the speech contest incident. In 1966—the haircut argument. The drinking bottomed out early in 1967. Something else might have happened—it seemed like a strong possibility. The question was not what happened. The question was—did I really want to know? I set the thought aside for the time being and decided to try to level off my life for a bit.

For about a month things seemed to quiet down. I was working for Timothy—helping repair homes, and the physical labor was good for me. There was little stress each day, as I knew the task we'd be working on for the day, and I felt the sense of accomplishment that comes from completing jobs. Some days I'd be grouting tile in a bathroom, or waxing floors, and on other days I'd be outside cleaning yards, preparing and painting parts of a house as needed. It brought up none of the anxiety of finding a "career" job. I worked mostly alone so there was no people-interaction stress, and I felt good each night—tired from the day and a good day's work behind me. Things eased up a bit financially as I started getting paid, and I began to nick away at my outstanding debts. I updated my budget for living expenses and decided how much I could allot for paying bills, and it began to feel like I was getting some order back in my life. It was a good feeling.

One day I felt particularly connected to my immediate world as I scraped the paint from window frames, enjoying a beautiful, cool fall day. I became aware of a quiet noise in the background and realized I could clearly hear the breeze blowing through the large cottonwood trees in the yard. For some reason that sound, and the simple enjoyment of it, was very important to me. I seemed to be feeling life with a whole new intimacy, after coming so close to the precipice of wanting to end it all. How could I have considered never again being able to hear the hushed beauty of those blowing leaves? The stark insanity of the place I'd recently visited—mortality and the loss of it—came more clearly to me as I scraped dead paint.

One night I prayed:

"Father, I am ready. I have contemplated on a whole new level what it means to turn my will and life over to You. I have had control back for a week—I hate it. I no longer want life without You. I once again decide to turn my will and life over to You. You have given me the power to trust You completely. Thank you. You shielded me from the realization of my death wish feelings until the right time. Thank you. Give me the words to share this experience. It's a big one. Thank you for helping me reclaim the anger at Dad—the Dad of twenty years ago. Thank you for your mysterious ways. I don't know what's going on, but I feel myself changing."

I thought about Wayne for the first time in several weeks and the interaction that had brought me to that point. I felt once again strong enough in my destiny to be a writer that I knew Wayne's attempts to pull that away from me couldn't, wouldn't, and didn't work. How far had I come from the time just two years before, when I almost gave up on being a writer. My girlfriend at the time had asked to see a book I had written, and then she hadn't commented on it—it appeared she hadn't even read it. She put the manuscript I gave her on the mantle of her fireplace. It lay there, unopened, for several weeks, until I meekly retrieved it and thought I must not be much of a writer for her not to even read what I had written. I almost quit writing.

And yet now, Wayne's even more direct attempt, "*your goal of going to creative writing school is a fantasy*", had failed, and I felt stronger in my belief in myself as a writer than before. Now, how the heck had that worked? I marveled.

Several days later, the thought came to me that my intuition was correct to go talk to Wayne—just not for the reason I had thought. I had to be mistreated—put down, belittled, made to feel like who I was not—to be able to claim my anger toward my Dad, who had done the same thing to me many times when I was growing up. I had carried that anger for a long, long time, buried deeply, unable to release it—and I would have continued to do so—had the right button not been pushed.

As I thought about that over the weekend before Thanksgiving, the anger began to percolate to the surface and crystallize. I began to write. In my writing, I connected a certain kind of man, like Wayne, like Dad—who because of their pride needed to be the alpha male, and my suicidal feelings. My self caring and sense of worth had been robbed—mostly as a teenager, to the point where I felt I deserved to die—it became like a death wish. In that way, I made the connection between the talk I had with Wayne and the things that had happened with my Dad. I had thought I was through with old anger at my Dad. I really had. My ACA mentor, called a sponsor, had been prodding me for several years to see if there was any anger toward my Dad. I invariably swore that I had been angry, but I wasn't any more. I hadn't been able to see or sense any anger.

Yet now I could feel it. There was a smug arrogance about Wayne that resonated from childhood—I'm sure I'm right, I can do and say whatever I want and you have to believe it—because I say so. A moral superiority. I know what's best for you because I know more than you, and you can't be who you think you are—you have to be who I say you are.

It also resonated with the religious teachings Wayne and others offered—God is about love, was the stated message on one hand, but religion was about judging others so we could be better than them on the other hand. God loves you but you are flawed material, so you have to always work hard—to avoid going to hell. Was the message about the love of God or the fear of hell? It got all confused and mixed up in complicated interpretations of Bible verses that only seemed to make sense to the teacher. Something didn't add up about what had been presented of God to me, and I began to see the dysfunction—not in God, but in the way some men had presented God.

I got angry about it. It was the Monday before Thanksgiving. It was rainy and we had been scheduled to work outside, so I wasn't working that day. I sat in my apartment, feeling my anger rising to the surface. I was angry at my Dad—from childhood. I was angry at Wayne—for how he tried to rob my truth in the guise of being a loving "mentor." I was angry at religious teachers—at muddled messages about God and man. Suddenly I had to do something. I was sitting on my couch, looking across the room at my bookshelves. I saw several notebooks full of Bible study notes. I saw a big notebook labeled, "Institute in Basic Youth Conflicts," by Bill Gothard. This was a seminar on family living I had attended in the '70's, taught by a man who had never been married, which I had always thought was odd. It had been full of complicated, and I now believed dysfunctional, methods to get right with God. We were supposed to memorize a chapter of the Bible every week, to prove our sincerity to God—which I had tried unsuccessfully to do over one summer, only to feel like a failure and unworthy because I couldn't stand up to the task. Only later did I realize the task was unreasonable and burdensome.

I saw several Bible commentaries—which sometimes confused more than shed light— seeming to say, "This is what James really meant when he wrote this passage." Some supporting a Christian exclusivity that left the rest of the world on the outside when it came to being on a walk of faith. I found it puzzling how this Bible which taught love was used to promote so much condemnation—of the other world religions, and even of other Christian denominations. And how much time was devoted to proving the point.

The way God was portrayed confused me— not so much about love as about punishment, never being good enough, and obedience even when it didn't seem to make sense.

I looked at all those materials, suddenly leaped out of my chair, took down the Bible study notes, and began ripping them out of the notebook, shredding the pages and flinging them around in a fluttering cloud that drifted down to litter my living room floor. I took down the Gothard notebook—tore out and shredded those pages. I took several of the most "fundamentalist" Bible commentaries and tore the books apart.

Finally I felt physically spent. My anger was depleted for the moment, and I sat and contemplated what I had just done. It felt very freeing—I felt more free to seek God in a whole new and loving way. A God who wanted good and wonderful things for me. I felt a release from the God who was watching to punish me should I step off the narrow line of what was "acceptable,"—the God who wished me to fear Him—the God who treated me like my Dad had treated me, the God who talked like Wayne had talked to me. It felt marvelous as I sat there contemplating the inches deep litter of paper flooring my living room. It was a gloriously satisfying moment. I could almost visualize God smiling at my victory in understanding Him more fully. My breath slowed. I calmed and quietly sat with the feeling.

I was not to savor this experience for long. Several hours later, after I had cleaned up the paper and put it in the trash, I got the call. It was my sister, Susan,—"you better come home, Dad is dying."

Chapter 13

That evening I sat numbly on a plane headed for Tulsa, Oklahoma, knowing that what I had expected and dreaded for several years had finally happened. Also knowing in some deep intuitive way that my life had, in the moment of that phone call, changed forever. As I looked around the dimly lit cabin, muted conversations around me, the pain was very near the surface. Random thoughts ran through my head, jumbled up and competing for my attention. He had no right to die now—it was too soon. We had just started getting close—like I had wanted to do for years, but somehow could never make happen. I thought back to my sister's wedding the previous February when we awkwardly hugged—for the first time I could ever remember. I thought back to my Dad loaning me money—when I got brave enough to ask for his help. Then there were the phone calls he'd made to check up on me— just because I'd asked. "Dad, I know you've said you want to stay out of my world and not be a bother. But I'd really like it if you would call occasionally and ask how I'm doing." For the past year, he had done just that—and it felt wonderful. He would just listen as I told him about the events of my world. It had been so special. The last time I had seen my Dad—in September, at an ACA retreat—he and my Mom came down from Tulsa to a camp outside Houston to see my world—my ACA world—just because I had asked them. I slept in the same cabin with my Dad, we ate meals together, and he met my people. On Sunday morning before they left, in the cafeteria, in front of everyone, in front of all of my ACA friends, he hugged me. I cherished that moment. I wondered if it would ever happen again.

But it was not a surprise that this trip was happening. I had been anticipating and, in a way, preparing for this moment for a long time. I had known that I would eventually get the phone call, the one I had gotten this evening. Back in 1985, I was dating a woman named Sheila, and she had helped me face what I knew would happen—that my Dad would die early. We talked a lot about what I could see happening with him, how it would feel when it did happen, and how I would handle it. I thought I was fairly well prepared—but I wasn't.

My Dad had a long history of health problems. He had his first heart attack in 1974—when he was 44. I remembered visiting him in the hospital in Enid, Oklahoma and shaking his hand—his grip, normally strong and firm, was kitten soft, so frail. It shocked me deeply. Then he had open-heart surgery around 1979. It was deeply disturbing to see him in the hospital again, this time in Tulsa, Oklahoma, weakened and fragile. He had a colostomy in the early '80's, and when I came home for the holidays I would watch him gingerly walking around the house with a bag attached to his waist. He had a history of high blood pressure, and he was a smoker for many years, though he eventually quit for a while.

Even though he had sobered up in 1967 and began attending A.A., there seemed to be a lot bubbling within him, below the surface, that he just couldn't get to or resolve and I had long thought he would not live to be very old. In the early '80s, I was home for Christmas when "On Golden Pond" came on television, and the family gathered in the living room to watch it even though we'd seen it before. It came to the part where the Henry Fonda character thought he was having a heart attack and dying, lying on the front porch of the lake cabin. Moments before the scene began, my Dad got up and left the room. I think he knew something—that he would be visited by a scene like that.

I had come home to visit for Thanksgiving of 1985 and was sitting in the living room late one evening when the phone rang. It was my Dad, who had gone out to a meeting, and returning on icy roads, had been part of a multi-car pile-up. He was unhurt but asked me to come get him. I drove to the wreck site. I saw his pickup, totally crunched and dented, and knew he was lucky to have escaped alive. I saw the look in his eyes—he knew it too; I saw an awareness of his own mortality after the near miss. We were both awake late that night, restless, unable to sleep, sitting in the living room watching late night TV, not talking, but both very reflective. Death had sent us a warning signal and we both knew it.

From all of those things I had known my Dad would die early and that I should begin to prepare for it.

The next year when I came home for Thanksgiving, my Dad had started smoking again. I was horrified, and it confirmed my worst fears about the direction of his health. He had stopped smoking—but only briefly. I recovered from my shock, and later that evening,—because I needed to for me—I said to him, "Dad, when I walked in and saw you smoking a cigarette, it felt like I was seeing you with a drink in your hand." He didn't respond but became very quiet. He didn't quit smoking, and I knew it was only a matter of time. In some strange way it felt like he was committing slow suicide. I didn't know why. With his health history, it was insane for him to be smoking—and I really understood that in the moment of seeing him with a cigarette. My Dad smoking had been an indelible memory since childhood and this just continued the pattern.

As the plane began its descent into Tulsa, I prayed. "Please God, don't take my Dad. I worship him. I want to spend time with him. Now I know and feel that he really loves me. Don't take him away. Let him live."

It hurt. It felt like part of me was dying. It felt like too much. I had just come out of the deep, deep valley of my own death wish feelings, had started to get balanced, and now might have a whole new grief process to go through. We had just made it—it wasn't fair! Damn it God, was I in some kind of loop of endless losses? What was the deal? Did God have it in for me? The pain bubbled up close to the surface as the plane touched the ground, rolled the runway and taxied to the terminal. I knew it would all become real now and the feelings would hit, and I dreaded it— I dreaded the whole process I was embarking on.

Numbly I watched the cabin door open, not wanting to get off the plane, waiting until people cleared out, then woodenly walking into the terminal, seeing my sister Susan's tear-reddened eyes. We hugged long and walked out of the airport, saying little at first until we got to the car.

"So, where is he?"

"At Saint Anthony's, in ICU."

"What's the situation?" I knew I'd get the truth—Susan was a nurse—she would know.

"It's not good. They have him on a ventilator. The machine is breathing for him."

"What happened to him?"

"I think it was a stroke, but they don't know exactly for sure yet. He and Mom were at home and he suddenly lay down on the living room floor and became unconscious. Mom called 911, tried CPR until the ambulance got there."

"Is he awake?"

Out of the corner of my eye, I could see her look over at me. "No, he's still unconscious. I just want to warn you, he may not come out of it. The doctors have already been talking to Mom about turning off the machines. He's essentially brain dead already." As if she knew this was all I could handle, she stopped talking and we rode in silence toward town.

Finally we pulled into a parking lot, got out and walked up to the front of Saint Anthony's Hospital. I vaguely noted a tall building, which in the lights around it looked pink, but surely that was my imagination. We walked through the front doors, went into an elevator, rode it up, got off and went down a series of confusing long hallways—day bright from fluorescent lights—through tunnels of pastel walls, tile floors, sterile feel, the vague smell of disinfectants. Then we came to a nurse's station for ICU where I saw and hugged my mother, pain written deeply on her face. An ICU nurse talked to me to prepare me to face my father in a hospital bed with a tube down his throat, IV in his arm, monitors and machines all around. She looked at me in concern, "Are you ready to see your father?"

I took a deep breath, nodded and we went in to his room. It was dim compared to the hallway—muted lights turned low. He lay under a tan hospital blanket, not moving, his chest rising and falling in rhythm to the machines. Even prior visits to hospitals to see my Dad hadn't prepared me. At least then he had been conscious. Now he lay passive, seemingly asleep, yet eerily already looking dead. There—the word hit my brain. He was dead—not alive, not with us anymore, unable to tell me he loved me one last time—death was calling, death had visited. I could sense it, feel it at a visceral level—the father I had known had already left, his spirit raised, never to return, machines notwithstanding. My Dad's body lay there, but my Dad was already gone.

I stood there for another few seconds then a rush of pain too deep to express overcame me and I had to leave. I know we left the hospital and drove to my parent's house, but I didn't remember the drive. We sat at the house for a while, each of us encased in our own self protective cocoon, not speaking much. We knew we faced the decision to turn off the machines and let my Dad pass naturally and peacefully, but it was too much to talk about now. Tomorrow would be too soon—but it would have to suffice. We went to bed, and I slept a turbulent, uneasy sleep, full of dreams I could not remember the next morning.

\

CHAPTER 14

The next day, the Tuesday before Thanksgiving, the family needed to talk—to face death. The night before, my Mom had been told by the medical staff that my Dad was essentially brain dead. The only thing keeping him alive was the hospital equipment—the respirator was breathing for him. They were doing that because if we allowed it, the hospital wanted to harvest his organs. So we needed to decide. There was really no point in leaving him on machine life-support for much longer, but our permission was necessary for them to stop. Breakfast that morning was a morose affair. We fixed the meal and ate it mostly in silence. By that point, all three of my sisters had come to town, and along with my Mother, we talked—sitting at the table after the meal, and it wasn't a long conversation.

My Mom said, "So you all know the situation—Dad's being kept alive by the machines, and the hospital has recommended we stop the machines and let nature take its course."

I looked at my sister, Susan, needing the informed opinion of the nurse, not the sister.

"So what will happen when they turn off the machine?"

She gave a small shake of her head. "He's really gone already, so when they turn off the respirator, he will likely pass within a few minutes."

I nodded mutely, hearing what my gut had already told me. Kitty asked, "So he's really about to die? No chance otherwise?"

Susan just shook her head. Kitty's eyes filled with tears, and she silently wept. Nancy sat numbly silent. I felt more numb than sad, unable to cry.

"What about organ donation?" my Mom asked.

We looked at each other. I turned to Susan, "What would that mean?"

"Well, while they still had him on life support, they would take lungs, eyes, kidneys, anything they could give to someone else."

That seemed a barbaric mutilation of my father and I had a vivid mental picture, much too clear, of what it would look like. I shook my head, as the others looked at me. "I know the organs would do good for other people, but I just can't see doing that to Dad."

Mom and my sisters all seemed relieved and nodded their heads in agreement.

"Where did Dad want to be buried?" I asked, "Back in Texas?"

"No," my Mom replied, "he wanted to be cremated."

"Then that's what we should do," I replied.

We then got up from the table and quickly began to clear the breakfast dishes so each of us could go off to different parts of the house for a while and be alone.

Several hours later, we were gathered in the ICU at Saint Anthony's, where we were escorted into what a small sign by the door labeled as the "Grief Room." A nurse came and talked to us, to ask our wishes. My Mom confirmed that we wished to end life support. The nurse then escorted the whole family into his room, to see him one last time. As we stood there watching the machines push air into his lungs, I was once more struck by the feeling that his essence, his soul, had already gone and that this felt more like a wake than a visitation. The nurse suggested we leave for a moment so they could pull the tube out of his throat, and then we could return. We stepped out to the nurse's station and a few minutes later, the nurse called us back in.

When I saw my Dad this time, his functions were stopping, and we watched the last moment of his dying, as his breathing gradually came to a halt, as his chest stopped moving. My sisters and my Mom were crying, but I couldn't cry. I was sad, but no tears came. We stood there for a while and then the rest of the family was ready to leave, which they did. I wanted one last moment and stood there next to his bed, looking down at him. I reached out my hand, hesitated, then stroked his forehead—something I would never have thought of doing while he was alive. His skin felt cool, clammy, almost like wax—an unnatural texture. I stood there for a few moments, then left. I never saw my Dad's body again; it was absorbed by the death processes of the hospital. It was disquieting—I didn't have enough time to get used to the reality, the finality, of his death. The nurse, now carrying a clipboard, stopped me in the hall and asked me if the family would like to agree to organ donation. I shook my head and said we had decided against doing that. She looked disappointed but didn't press the point, and she left.

I went back into the Grief Room, where my sisters and Mom were quietly crying together, alone. The hospital staff was not around, which seemed odd—and there was no one to help us in the transition. I ached, and I could feel the hurt just under the surface, but there was something else to be done and it seemed like I was the one to do it. I called a funeral home, and began making arrangements for my Dad to be cremated. It felt like I had taken myself out of a grief place, but maybe taking action was part of my adjustment to the fact—my Dad was dead.

We stayed at the hospital for a while longer and then my sisters went home, and Mom and I went to the funeral home to finalize the cremation arrangements. The time at the funeral home was a blur, as I was ready to stop and be quiet for a while. Fortunately it didn't take long and I breathed a big sigh as we walked out into the afternoon sun, glad to have that part behind me. My Mom and I went to a Black-Eyed Pea for a late lunch and then we drove home.

My Mom got on the phone to begin the process of telling their out-of-town friends that Dad had died. People they knew in Tulsa had apparently gotten word passed around so she was just calling people they didn't see regularly.

I don't remember where my sisters were for the rest of that afternoon, or much of what I did. I sat on the back porch for a while, numb, not thinking, just trying to wrap my head around it. I looked up occasionally at the wooden porch cover my Dad and I had built several years before, and it only hurt to be reminded of that shared time. People kept stopping by, bringing food, and we had plenty to eat that night, but I wasn't really very hungry.

CHAPTER 15

By Wednesday morning, I was feeling closed in and overwhelmed by all that was happening. I needed a little breathing space, but I also had something I wanted to do. After breakfast, I got in my Dad's pickup and drove down to St. John's Hospital to see where Dad had worked the last two years of his life.

He had been an oilfield salesman for as long as I could remember—for about 30 years. But then, in the early '80's, the oil industry had taken a downturn and he had finally gotten out of the business. I think he had been laid off, but I never really knew for sure. He had started working at the Alcohol and Chemical Dependency Unit at St. John's, something about intake assessments and apparently some group monitoring—I wasn't sure about exactly what he had been doing—I'd never asked.

Mom had called a man named Mel who Dad worked for at the unit, and Mel had said if I wanted to come down, he'd be glad to show me around. As I drove across Tulsa, it was grey and overcast, and the fall leaves were gorgeous—ranging from bright orange to muted amber. Normally I would really enjoy the sight, but now they only reinforced that something had died.

I parked at the hospital and sat for a minute, steeling myself, knowing that I would have a strong reaction to seeing this aspect of my Dad's life. I got out, walked into the hospital, and after a bit of fumbling and hall walking, found the unit and Mel, a kindly grey-haired gentleman. He greeted me warmly and walked me through the unit, explaining the different aspects of their treatment program, and finally, he told me about my Dad.

"Ben was one of the first people that a new patient encountered on the unit. Right after the intake assessment, your Dad would explain to the patient what was going to happen while they were here and have them sign some preliminary paperwork. All the patients loved him, and related well to him."

"I'd never heard about this," I replied. "He never said anything about what he did here."

"I'm not surprised—that's the way your Dad was—he was pretty modest. Did you know about his barbecues for the patients? Out at his pecan grove?"

"I had heard something about that—from Mom."

"He would invite everyone out to his land, staff and patients, and we'd all go out in hospital vans, and he'd cook for us. The patients loved the barbecues—a chance to get away from the hospital, to be out in nature for a while. I think it was very healing for them."

I nodded, trying to get a picture in my mind.

"And here is his office." We walked inside a small office, fairly typical, and after standing in the doorway for a moment, I walked around behind his desk. I could see four letters with my Dad's signature on them, and the familiar handwriting gave me a jolt.

"Sit, if you'd like," Mel said.

I tentatively sat down in the desk chair, where my Dad had spent his last working hours.

"We're all in shock, you know. It still hasn't sunk in that he is gone," Mel gently said. "He saved a lot of lives with his work in A.A."

I nodded, mumbled a thank you, deeply touched, but unable to speak. I sat there for a few more moments then we walked back out into the hall. I had to leave, and I could sense Mel would understand.

"Thanks for showing me around, Mel. I really do appreciate it."

"I'm more than glad to do it, Dan. Take good care of yourself. This is going to be a tough time for a while."

"Yes, I understand. Well, thanks again." I shook his hand, turned and walked quickly down the hall and out of the hospital.

Dad's land. I suddenly knew I wanted— needed—to go out there. He had bought five acres on the east side of Tulsa, land that backed up to a creek and had some pecan trees on it. He had enjoyed being out there a great deal, and I knew some part of him was still out there. I got into his pickup, drove east out Highway 44, exited near Catoosa, went down a farm-to-market road, across an old two lane bridge, pulled up at the gate to his land. I was surprised at how easily I found it. I hadn't been out there in a while.

The key to the padlock on the gate was on the same ring as his truck keys, so I got out, unlocked the gate and swung it open. I drove through and into the glade where he spent so much time. There was a barbecue pit, a picnic table and several lawn chairs. I got out and just stood there for a moment. I was in a cleared space shaded by large trees, and further back was a dense grove of trees and quite a bit of underbrush. If you walked directly away from the road, picking through the underbrush, about 400 yards, the property ended at a bluff falling down to a small creek. My Dad had wanted to eventually clear the land of the underbrush and some old dead trees, but hadn't gotten a chance to do that.

I sat in one of the lawn chairs and thought about the last time we had come out here. It had been about two years ago. We had started with breakfast at a small coffee shop next to the highway, and I had tried to explain to him some of the things I was trying to work through in ACA—things that had happened in my teen years—some of them having happened with him. I lightly touched the subject and could see him looking pained and uncomfortable, so I veered away from that.

"Son, if you feel you must go back and relive what happened when you were growing up, do what you must. But if you just want to gripe about your childhood, I really don't want to listen to it. I sometimes get the feeling that you think Mom and I didn't do anything right, and I don't want to hear that."

"Sure Dad, I understand and I can honor that. It's not about griping though, for me anyway. It's about trying to let it all go." I could see he was uncomfortable with that whole line of thought, and I mentally decided not to bring it up again. But I also could somehow tell he didn't understand what I was trying to do. Now I sat and listened to the breeze blowing through the cottonwoods, and I wondered about that conversation. It struck me—not for the first time—that it was possible he didn't remember most, if not all, of what had happened between him and me. I was only recently beginning to remember, and at the time those things happened, he was drinking heavily. Maybe he just didn't remember and felt awkward because of it. And now I couldn't ask him and would never really know.

I shook myself, got up, and walked a bit further into the edge of the cleared area. I could see places where he had cleared some underbrush and some pecan trees with twigs grafted into them that were evidence of his work. I had come out to help him graft that last time, and I had watched him as he worked and explained to me what he was doing.

I hadn't felt like doing any grafting myself and didn't want to just stand around, so I had asked him if there was anything I could do. He pointed to several dead trees and said they needed to be cut down and burned—they were too close to the barbecue area, and he didn't want dead branches falling on anyone. I had taken his chain saw and, just by intuition, tried to figure out the best way to drop those trees. I finally got them cut down, sawed them up in sections, and burned most of the wood from them as my Dad worked further back in the grove, grafting sprigs. We worked steadily and long, and about mid-afternoon, we sat down in the lawn chairs to take a break and for him to have a cigarette.

He began telling me some story—I forget about what—something that had happened in his past. He told stories often, and at length. Sometimes I enjoyed them, and sometimes the telling felt a bit tedious and like the story was a wall between us, not a place where we connected. My Mom had told me that the men's group he facilitated in the evening at St. John's had confronted him about the story telling. They told him it felt like he was hiding himself from the group behind the stories. I felt the same way and spoke up.

"You know, Dad, you tell stories a lot, and sometimes they're really good, but sometimes I just don't want to listen. So I guess I just need to say, with any other adult male, if I didn't want to listen, I'd get up and walk away. So I guess I'm saying, if I feel like I need to, I'll just walk away here too."

He said nothing, just nodded in response, and we sat quietly after that. He didn't tell any more stories.

Now as I stood in the glade on his land, I could hear more anger—more hostility—in what I had said than I was aware of at the time. I realized it must have hurt my Dad for me to say that—it would have hurt me if someone had said it to me. And now I could never take it back. My throat closed up tight with a big lump in it, but tears would not come. I stood there for a long moment living the pain of my regret. The pain subsided for the moment, but I knew it hadn't gone away.

Suddenly, I needed to do something, and I knew what it had to be. Dad's pickup had a toolbox in the bed, where he kept his tools and gear. I unlocked and opened it, got out his work boots, took off my tennis shoes and pulled on the boots. I took out his work gloves and pulled them on, moving purposefully and with assurance. I took out his chain saw, carried it to the back of the glade, past the ashes and residue that still lingered from the earlier trees I had cut and burned. I looked up and around, picked three dead trees. I set down the chain saw, pulled the cord, and fired it up. Very deliberately I made a cut on the first tree, then a deeper one further up on the other side. It weakened, began to sway, and finally fell with a loud crash. I repeated the process twice more and was left with three dead trees lying in along the ground in different directions, crushing the underbrush. I stood and looked at them for a few minutes, and it became more real—my Dad is dead.

I decided to come back later in the week to cut up and burn the trees—I needed to feel and sense what I had told myself by cutting down those trees. I carried the chainsaw back and put it into the toolbox, stripped off the gloves, changed out of the boots, and put them back as well. I stood and looked out over his land for a long moment. I could see where the underbrush was mashed down from the trees I had cut. I could hear the breeze through the trees—the quiet intensified after the racket of the chainsaw. Somehow I knew I had done what I was supposed to do there. I got in the pickup, pulled out next to the road, and went back and locked the gate. I looked back once at the picnic table and lawn chairs, looking forlorn and abandoned. Then I drove away, in pained regret at the words I had said to my Dad, that I could never take back.

Chapter 16

Wednesday night, I went through my parent's financial papers. Mom had asked if I would do that to determine where she was from a money standpoint. Dad had handled all of those issues, and she wasn't sure how safe she was financially. I spread their papers on the dinner table and began to go through them. My sister Kitty sat down across from me, wanting to support me in some way. I asked her to give me a little space, and she looked hurt and got up and left. I've since regretted having to do that, but couldn't see myself being able to complete that difficult task with her hovering over me.

I spent about two hours going over my parent's financial life and was struck by two things—first, my Dad had left Mom in pretty good shape financially. The second thing I noted was pretty eerie. My Dad had organized their financial papers well; they were easy to follow, and thorough. It was not like the papers of someone who has ongoing affairs—sort of messy and needing a little cleanup. These papers were neat and well ordered—as if he knew someone would have to come along behind him to take over the recordkeeping. They were the papers of a person who knew he wouldn't have a chance later to organize them.

I gave Mom my evaluation that she was in pretty good shape financially and commented on how orderly the papers were. She was not surprised, and said she'd gotten a feeling that on some level Dad had known he might not have much longer. She said he had spent a lot of time in the last year straightening up the elements of his world. It was a shock to me to see such strong evidence that my Dad knew he would die early—and soon. It made me very aware that I wanted to work hard so that I wouldn't die before my time. Recovery, for me, was a life or death issue—if I didn't want to die early like Dad.

The rest of Wednesday evening was quiet. While I had been out at the land, I had gotten a lot of messages of support from people in Houston, and I was hugely gratified and deeply honored by all the caring. Tom, the youth minister from my church, called that evening. We had worked together on the senior high youth ministry from 1982 to 1985—I had sat in his office many times and we had talked about the ministry and life in general. He had been the first one to suggest I seek counseling help, and it was a great suggestion. His call meant a great deal to me because I felt he understood a lot about the struggles I had been going through. Some old friends I had known since high school called, expressing condolences. I was very touched that lots of people from ACA called—they had heard me talk in meetings about my struggles with my Dad, and remembering painful things from my childhood. Denise, a woman I had been deeply involved with the previous year, had called. That was awkward—I appreciated her support but we hadn't been talking much, there was still some residual energy from when we dated, and it was a strained conversation. By the end of the evening, I was trying to absorb all the warmth and support, but it was difficult because of the amount and power of the support focused on me.

Thanksgiving was, of course, subdued. I don't even remember the turkey dinner, but I think we had one. I got one call from a group of people from ACA who were having Thanksgiving dinner together. One after the other, they got on the phone to offer me their condolences and support. It was hugely touching—it almost left me breathless.

About mid-afternoon, I left to go meet with the minister who was to lead Dad's memorial service. Dad had been cremated, so there would be no burial service, but we had agreed we wanted to have a ceremony of some sort. We decided to go ahead and have it on Friday, the day after Thanksgiving, but we were aware that being in the middle of a holiday, there might not be a lot of people who could attend. However, we felt it was better to go ahead and have a small service rather than wait.

I drove over to the small Presbyterian Church where the service would be held. It was a sentimental choice, because Mom and Dad's home A.A. meeting was held at that church—a group they had helped to get started. The minister was also in 12 Step, and having known my Dad, had gladly agreed to do the service. I'd never met him before, but he was a young, warm, caring man, and I knew we'd be in good hands. We laid out a simple service: an introduction, a couple of songs, a eulogy, and closing remarks.

Wednesday evening, Mom and the sisters and I had sat down to discuss what we'd like to have in his memorial service. They had turned to me and by consensus had asked if I would deliver the eulogy. I agreed, and it never occurred to me that it would be otherwise. Then it came to picking the music, and I'm not sure who suggested it, maybe Mom, but we decided upon two Frank Sinatra songs—"That's Life" and "My Way." We all had smiled as those choices were made, because the songs seemed to capture an essence of Dad. It seemed to the family that it was a perfect selection—we couldn't imagine it any other way.

Yet now, when I mentioned those songs to the minister, he frowned and seemed to hesitate.

"Are you sure you want to use those songs?"

"Yes," I said, puzzled. "Why wouldn't we?"

"Well, I guess I'm just thinking in terms of recovery and the 12 steps—we don't really do things 'my way,' but we do it the way the book and the program tell us to."

"Yes, I see your point, but I think this speaks more to style and lifestyle than to any adherence to a program. My Dad had his own way about him, and that's what we're really trying to honor by that song."

I could see he remained unconvinced, but I knew that for my family's sake, it was important for that song to be part of the service.

"So you want to go ahead and use 'My Way'?"

"Yes, sir, I do."

He acquiesced with our wishes, and we moved on. I let him know I'd be doing the eulogy, and we wrapped up our planning. He suggested I meet him in a small room behind the altar, and we would come out together after people were seated, to signal the start of the service. I agreed, we shook hands, and I left and drove home.

I spent that evening jotting some notes on what I would say. My Mom had suggested I introduce myself as Ben's son, since a lot of people from Tulsa might not know who I was. I agreed and mentally hoped Mom wouldn't be too disappointed if not a lot of people were able to attend. Mom and the sisters left the rest of the talk up to me. I had been doing a lot of public speaking around that time, so the speaking part was comfortable. But speaking about my Dad this soon after his death—that was something altogether different. I didn't know if I could do it. I decided to plan my talk around the three parts of Step 12 of the A.A. program, because I felt that was an accurate characterization of what my Dad was all about. How I would do trying to speak those words? I wasn't really sure, and I prayed for strength sufficient to the task.

Chapter 17

I don't remember what time of day we decided to hold the service, but I'm thinking it may have been around 1 p.m. I don't remember much about that morning—was it cloudy, sunny, rainy, cold? I didn't notice. I just remember going through the motions of showering, putting on my suit, and driving to the church with Mom and the sisters. I split off from them and went and met the minister in the little alcove room behind the altar. We had gotten there early, so only a few people had arrived. The minister and I sat quietly, not talking, as organ music began in prelude to the service. Finally, the minister got some signal that it was time, and he and I stood and walked into the sanctuary. I paused in my stride, jolted like a physical impact, when I saw that the church was completely full, with people standing in the back. It was a small church, but there must have been 300 people packed in there. It took my breath away to realize that this many people had interrupted their holiday weekend to come honor my father.

We sat down where the ministers normally sit, behind the pulpit, facing the audience. On the first row, on the right side, were my Mom and sisters, my grandmother, and several of my aunts and cousins. I recognized a few of the other people, but the rest of the crowd was unknown to me. I assumed they were from A.A. The minister went to the pulpit and welcomed everyone to the memorial service for Ben Hays as I sat, somewhat in shock, trying to absorb the size of the crowd. He made a few introductory remarks and then sat down as "That's Life" began playing. I looked down and saw my Mom smiling as the music played. The song finished, the minister went back up, read a scripture, and then introduced me.

As I stood, a calm fell over me, and I knew I would be able to do this thing—I would be able to speak the words I had prepared. I stepped up to the pulpit.

"Hello, my name is Dan Hays. Ben Hays was my father." I noticed in a detached sort of way that my voice was strong, calm and warm. "On behalf of my family and myself, I'd like to welcome you all here today. We are deeply touched that you join us here today to celebrate the life of Ben Hays." I looked out and could see sympathetic eyes wherever I looked, all focused on me. A few tears were beginning to well up in the audience.

"The large number of people here today is a testimony to the number of lives my father touched. A number of people this week have told me how much my Dad had an influence on their lives. By this I know he carried the message." I could feel my throat clutch up. "My Dad and I had a great deal of healing over the last several years of his life. By this I know he practiced the principles. If you ever saw my Dad out at his land, grafting pecan trees, or just sitting and enjoying the breeze," a number of smiles at this, "you would know he had had a spiritual awakening. And if you've ever seen those checked tennis shoes he wore," big smiles now, and a lot of laughter—the shoes were hideously ugly, "you know that he had learned not to take himself too seriously. My Dad had a lot of courage—at one point he lost it all, job, family, home, but he persevered and put it all back together. The songs we selected today were appropriate to my Dad, because he did do things his own special way. I'm very proud of my father," my throat almost closed—edge of tears—almost lost it. "Peace be with you, Ben." I sat down, not able to look at my family, instead staring at a spot above the crowd at the back of the church. The minister stepped up, made a few closing remarks, and dismissed the gathering to muted organ music.

After the service, several people came up and thanked me for what I had said. One man even said in all seriousness, that my Dad had saved his life. Those words impacted me deeply, because I knew he meant it literally, yet at the time I could only nod and mumble a thanks.

We went over to the house of one of my parent's friends for what I guess you would call a wake, but I don't remember much about it. I visited with relatives, talked to people, and tried to calm down after what I had just been through. Finally, the family went home, and we were quiet and pretty subdued.

There didn't seem to be much left to do in Tulsa, so the next day, I took a plane flight back home. I didn't realize until later that I had forgotten to go back to my Dad's land, cut up and burn the trees I had cut down. I must have known that doing that would be too much to handle right then.

Chapter 18

For several weeks, I thought the grief process about losing my Dad was not going to be too bad. I was working for Timothy still, doing handyman jobs at various locations. The physical labor felt good, as well as allowing me some time to reflect, during repetitive tasks. I thought a lot about my Dad.

When I was about 8 or 9, we had moved to Farmington, and my Dad and I spent a lot of time together. Later, that wouldn't be the case, but at the time, it felt quite nice. He was a salesman for an oilfield service company and had to make calls at well sites. Sometimes I would be allowed to go with him, and it was a real treat—I would have to get up very early on a Saturday morning, but it was worth it. I remembered the smell of fresh coffee as he poured a cup from his thermos, and the words coming from the radio in Navajo, because that was the only channel on at 5:30 a.m. I slept a lot as he drove, but then would groggily wake as he nudged me when we approached the location. It was very exciting to me to be on a rig site, especially if my Dad was there when they were about to fracture or acidize a well. There would be a lot of extra trucks around, the noise was overwhelming, and the whole thing was very exciting.

I felt special, since I was usually the only child around. The service hands from my Dad's company were very protective of me, but sometimes they would play tricks on me. Like the time they were about to perforate the well. In that operation they set off charges on the end of a wire line deep within the earth, at the bottom of a well bore. They told me to go outside their truck and hold on to the line so I could feel when the charge went off, but to hold on tight because it would shake me around quite a bit. I did, and they must have had a great laugh at the sight of me hanging on for dear life, expecting a thrill ride. I felt a minor tremor, which they told me was the charge going off. They kidded me about it, but with a lot of affection.

One time, Dad told me that one of the rig hands had discovered an Indian site on a bluff high above the location, and there was even some old Indian corn scattered around. He knew I loved to explore, so when the man pointed out a small niche under an overhang in the bluff, I quickly scampered up and found the site. There were some small dried up kernels of corn around a rudimentary campsite, and the discovery was very exciting and amazing.

As I looked down, I could see the whole drill site laid out below me—the rig, pump trucks, tank trucks, cars and pickups, and from my perspective high above it, I felt like the king of it all. I could see my Dad and several men down below looking up at me, and I waved to them. I climbed down the bluff, began running toward a flat piece of ground, when my Dad ran toward me, waving at me to stop. He yelled across that I should throw a rock on the flat ground, and when I did, it sank from sight with a plop. I had been about to run across the slurry pit for the used drilling mud—a muddy pond, but crusted on top, making it look solid. My stomach sank at the thought of falling into that muck. I sheepishly waved at Dad and walked around the pit, grateful at how he had saved me.

I was painting that morning, and I chuckled to myself as I dipped my brush for more paint, at how shocked I would have been to fall into that mud. That was almost as funny as Jackson's Lake. It was a small lake outside Farmington and Dad and I would go fishing there occasionally. We'd rent a small boat and motor out to the middle of the lake, then drop a couple of lines in the water. I was about 10 at the time. One time my boredom kicked in, and I asked Dad if it was a lake you could swim in.

"Sure, son, you can swim if you want. Go ahead." He didn't mention the fact that if I were to go thrashing around in the water it would likely ruin the fishing. I don't think he was that committed as a fisherman anyway.

A sudden thought occurred to me. "But there are fish in that water, right?"

"That's why we're here," he said with a smile.

"Will they bite me?"

"Son, I think the fish will be more scared of you than you are of them."

I wasn't so convinced of that. I sat and thought about it all for a minute.

"But I don't want to get my clothes all wet."

"Strip down and swim in your underwear."

I blanched at the thought, but then looked around. The only sign of life was at the small dock in the far distance. I couldn't think of any other objections, and felt like I had committed myself when I asked about swimming, so I reluctantly began to peel off my clothes. Images of the murky darkness underneath the boat ran through my head, little fishes waiting to chew my toes. Finally, I stood on the bow of the boat in my underwear, breathing deeply, then I just jumped off the boat. I was an excellent swimmer, and spent most of the summer in the public pool in town, but this wasn't about swimming. I had also seen monster movies like "The Blob," with Steve McQueen, and "Creature from the Black Lagoon." Suddenly this was about the monsters laying in wait in the blackness of the water. As I hit the water, I was turning back toward the boat, paddling to grasp it as quickly as possible and pull myself up and in and out of danger's way.

My Dad sat there watching me, a squint on his face as he tried not to grin.

"So, is that all you're going to swim?"

"Yeah, Dad, I think I've had enough."

"OK, then." He handed me a towel and turned back to his fishing, to let me regain my composure and a bit of dignity.

For some reason, I thought of the building projects. When I was in my 20's, Dad and I had built a trellis along one side of a back porch of a house we were living in, so my Mom could have some privacy. Another time, I believe it was about the fall of 1981, Dad had decided to build a cover for the back porch of their house in Tulsa. It was to be a pretty substantial cover, anchored by 4 by 4 posts at the outer corners, then more 4 by 4s running from the corners and connecting it to the roof. We designed it, did all our measurements very carefully, and spent a couple of days cutting lumber. We cemented the posts in, and when we set the cross members in place from the roof and from corner to corner, nothing fit right. It was all off by about 4 inches, and we were horrified, thinking we'd have to do everything over. Then we realized we had put the cross members on top of the corner post in the wrong order. When we switched them, everything suddenly fit perfectly in place. We laughed long and hard about that, spiced with relief that we had not made a major mistake.

The thoughts seemed to flow in no time sequence or order, because next I remembered the time he wanted me to give blood with him. I was about 17, we lived in Fort Worth, and he asked me to go run and errand with him. I went along, not knowing where we were going, and was puzzled when he pulled up into the parking lot of a hospital. He said he was going to give blood for a friend who was having surgery. He looked at me expectantly, and I was horrified to realize that he wanted me to donate also.

"So, do you want to give blood?" he asked.

"No, no, I don't," was all I could say, as I shook my head vigorously. I could see he was disappointed, but I didn't care. I had hated needles since I was a child and there was no way I was doing this. I sat in his car until he returned, the Band-Aid on his forearm mute evidence of his donation. We were silent driving home, and I was confused as to why he thought I would do what he had asked. Didn't he know I hated needles?

I frowned as I dipped the brush into the bucket and went back to work.

Later that week I remembered crossing the creek. When we were still living in Farmington, several times in my teens, Dad had taken me on hunting trips with a group of men. Those were terrible experiences for me—trying to sleep in a smoke-filled trailer as the men played poker and drank. Driving around in the cold, sitting in the back of a pickup with the other kids as the men sat in the warm cab drinking whiskey and looking for deer. So I had no fond memories of hunting, until this one.

I was about 19 and had come home from Texas Tech one weekend during hunting season. My Dad and I went down to Aunt Alta's farmhouse outside Waxahachie because she had access to a hunting lease we could use. We got up early and drove out to the lease, and began walking across the land. We came to a small creek—six inches deep, but about ten feet wide. I was wearing my waterproof boots, but my Dad had forgotten his boots and was wearing only tennis shoes. He would be miserable if he had to hunt in wet tennis shoes, so I carried him across the creek on my back, then went back for the rifles. It didn't seem like a big deal at the time, but later there seemed to be some sort of symbolic significance to that act. My Dad crystallized it about a year before he died when he told me, "When you did that, it really hit home for me that you had become a man." Exactly! That's why I had remembered that small incident for 20 years. It symbolized the time I was strong enough to carry my father's weight—to take on the load of being a man.

Why had I remembered that now? I couldn't remember what brought it up. I could tell how strong the memory was—my feet were cold, deathly cold. Granted, I was outside in December—but in Houston, and it was a relatively warm day. No, my feet were cold like they had felt while I was wading across that icy creek, the weight of my father on my back.

Chapter 19

The pain hit on December 14th. It was a rainy Monday, and I was working indoors for Timothy, because it was too wet to work outside. I didn't see the pain coming, and am not sure exactly what brought it on—maybe just enough time had passed for the numbness to have worn off. I was caulking the edge of a bathtub in a rent house when I had the thought that Dad wouldn't be with us for Christmas. Just like that, a physical pain hit me, and my whole body hurt violently, like I was in the middle of a car wreck. My shoulders ached, my neck was tight, my stomach hurt badly enough that I had to bend over. My chest ached—my whole core had a dull aching sensation. My Dad—was dead.

I sat down on the edge of the tub, unable to get up, hurting like hell and hoping it would subside soon. It didn't. I couldn't concentrate—the pain was everywhere and I couldn't think. After what seemed like hours but was probably about ten minutes, I realized on some deep level that this pain wasn't going to ease up for a while. I intuitively sensed that, and also I knew I couldn't work while I was in that condition. I went and found Timothy, who was startled at the strange expression on my face. I didn't want to try to explain, so I just told him I wasn't feeling very good, and needed to go home. He said I didn't look so good, and sure, I could go home. I could barely hear him as I stumbled out the door and somehow drove home.

I lay on my bed through most of the afternoon, and the pain settled in as a dull aching, but didn't seem about to diminish. I tried to call a number of people I knew in the ACA program, but no one was around. Finally, in desperation, I called a couple of people at their work locations, something I normally would not do. No one was there. I grew panicky, because it felt like the pain would never end, and I didn't know how long I could take it. The reality was stark and pure—my Dad was dead, and he was never coming back. Finally, I got through to someone. Suzanne, a woman I knew in ACA, answered her phone at work. She and I had talked right after Dad died, and she'd told me some things about how grief might come up.

"Suzanne, this is Dan."

"Hey guy, how are you doing? You sound strange."

"I'm not doing good, not good at all. You remember how you said the pain of my Dad would hit sooner or later?"

"Yes," she answered hesitantly, "has it hit?"

"Boy, has it. Big time! It is so bad I had to come home from work."

"Wow, that sounds pretty intense. What does it feel like? What's going on?"

"It doesn't feel like anything, just pain. It just hurts—all over. It's the damnedest thing I've ever experienced. I can't describe it, but it's bad enough that I've been laying on the bed doubled up all afternoon."

"Shit! Have you been crying?"

"That's what's really weird. It's like it hurts too bad to cry. It's too deep. Does that make any sense? It sounds really whacky when I say it."

"Not at all. It makes perfect sense. Right after your Dad died you had to go into hero mode—take care of the family, take care of the funeral. You never had a chance to have your feelings then, so they're hitting now. Don't worry, the tears will show up."

"So what do I do about it?"

"What you're really asking is—how do I make it go away? You can't—just like they're always saying, the way out is through. You have to just let this pain work its way through you and release. Avoiding it is what got us into ACA—because we never could release the old pains. And I suspect there might be some old pain mixed in with what you're feeling now. But if you don't let it out now, you'll just have to do it later." She paused, then continued, "I know that's probably not what you want to hear right now, but you know it's time. You're doing a really brave thing by facing the pain head on. Just don't do anything stupid, like getting drunk or anything."

"I won't. But promise me this won't last forever."

"It won't. It just feels like it will never end—but it will. Trust me, it will."

———————

I called Timothy the next morning and told him I wouldn't be coming to work that day, and spent the day lying on my bed, aching and hurting, curled up in a ball holding my stomach.

At one point in the afternoon, while the pain was at ebb, I called Sue and told her I had some deep grief to release. I thought I needed a good cry—but I didn't want to do it alone. I knew Sue from ACA and she felt safe—like I could have my feelings with her and she'd just be there for me. I asked if I could come over and watch "It's a Wonderful Life" with her. That movie had always touched my sentimental side, had father issues in it, and I suspected it would help the grief release. Sue agreed to let me come over, which I did, and it worked.

That evening I sat on her couch all knotted up as we watched the movie. When George Bailey started talking about how he wanted to leave Bedford Falls and how his Dad's life wasn't good enough, I lost it. I fell apart. I doubled over crying deeply as Sue held me. I didn't remember much of the rest of the movie—I was crying too hard. I sobbed deeply, wailing from down in the gut, bent over double, tears flowing intensely. When it settled some, for a moment, I realized that for years I had not given my Dad credit for what he had done—coming back from the alcoholism that had wrecked our family, sobering up and staying sober, putting his life and family back together. I cried again thinking about what he had accomplished, and I cried because I hadn't had a chance to tell him how proud of him I was. I finally settled down and stopped, limp and spent. I thanked Sue for being there for me, drove home, and barely got undressed before falling into a long, deep sleep.

The next day I was able to go to work, and could work a full day. I suspected it wasn't all over, but that there would be more feelings. But for now, after the deep cry of last night, the pain seemed to have subsided. That night at home, I began to write a poem about my Dad—just a couple of lines that fell out of my head onto paper, but I could sense there was more I needed to write. It was a poem about the things Dad had accomplished, and how I was proud of what he had done. I felt new perspective coming to me.

Then, just before I went to bed, an odd sensation hit. I felt a deep anger toward my Dad. I felt it, recognized it for what it was, and grew very uncomfortable with it. I wasn't sure why I was angry—but it felt disloyal. It just did. My Dad had just died—why would I be angry at him? But I had also seen something else—how deep and pure and hot that anger had been before I pushed it down. It was like looking into a furnace at a steel mill—almost white hot anger. It scared me. I wasn't sure what it was about, and I wasn't sure I wanted to know.

Chapter 20

Over the next several days, I worked on the poem about my Dad, adding new verses and refining the ones already written. It expanded into 16 verses, some folksy reminiscences about Dad, but several reflections about who I had realized my Dad really had been. Being involved in his funeral, having people from A.A. tell me about Dad had given me new perspective on him. I realized that this poem was something I'd like to share with the family.

Yet even with the reflections about Dad, my feelings were bouncing around a lot. It was like in the Three Stooges movies when Moe, Larry and Curly were all trying to get out the door at the same time, and they would get stuck—that's how my feelings were competing to get out. I'd feel tender and reflective as I remembered my Dad; I'd feel sad and pained at realizing more fully that he was no longer around, then the anger would surface. No, more than anger—that's what was puzzling to me. Part of me was furious with my Dad—it seemed to me he was a coward who never had the guts to make amends, to face the guilt and own up to what he did to me. And he died before he did. But he had 20 years when he was sober, and he never did. How could he not have taken a personal inventory on his family and his drinking? But he may not have. He damn sure didn't have the courage to face the "wreckage of the past." That pissed me off. The back and forth swing of feelings went on for several days, but the depth of the anger frightened and mystified me the most. Where was this coming from, and why now?

It welled up when I was driving north to Tulsa to be with the family for Christmas. I knew I wanted to be with family during the holiday, since it would be our first without Dad. Christmas had been especially about Dad because his birthday was on December 24th. I was on I-45 heading north from Houston, just passing Ennis, when I realized I was getting madder and madder. My face was flushed, my neck was bowed—tight as steel. My pulse rate was 76, which was high for me while sitting in a car. I kept visualizing boxing and going out of control and trading hard blows with someone. Suddenly I knew I was 16 years old, wanting to hurt someone. Physically abuse them, beat them. I could feel it deep in my soul, a need to lash out, to hurt—like I had been hurt?

I started to get vague fragments of memories. It was a cloudy, grey day as I drove north, but somehow I sensed it was once again about nighttime—cold, dark, nighttime. I had no memories of Christmas 1964 through 1966. Those years were a blank and from the memories I had gotten back, those were the years when the drinking and the abuse were both getting worse. So I reflected now as I drove through Dallas. Where was I on the Christmas I was 16? I would have been in Oklahoma City. We had moved from Farmington to Oklahoma City in October of 1966—we had been very suddenly and unexpectedly told we were moving, that Dad had been transferred. It was very traumatic for me, because I had grown up in Farmington, and had a known world, which was arbitrarily uprooted. As I drove I realized I hadn't thought about Oklahoma City for many years, the memory too painful. Only vague fragments of memories came back.

I remembered feeling isolated, being in a new school, the cold, cold overcast winter days, the strange house we had rented. There was some memory of Mom being in the hospital—in early December? I couldn't remember why. I flashed on painful memories of riding a school bus home, the outsider, sitting alone and talking to no one. I would get off the bus and walk three blocks through the neighborhood, back to the cold and lifeless house. Later I got a job—my first job—washing dishes and being a busboy at a hamburger restaurant down on the Northwest Freeway. I was really proud of that job—and then I wasn't proud, I wasn't working there, and the memory just blanked out.

Of course, I could remember the end of Oklahoma City—we had only lived there four months. Aunt Jean and Uncle Bill came and picked up my Mom, my sisters and me and what few possessions we could scoop up on the fly, and took us to Fort Worth to live with my grandmother. My Dad, who had lost his job due to the drinking, had been left behind, passed out drunk on the couch, as Mom could do nothing further for him. I had a mental image of my Dad lying there, awakening to an empty household, an empty bottle, and an empty future. The image had pained me for 20 years, and came up again now with full force.

I had always wondered what had happened to my Dad after we left. He disappeared for about a year, and I had heard something about him going off and working the wheat harvest, which he had done in college. I knew something had happened to him during that time, because the next year he came back to Fort Worth, sobered up, joined A.A., and began putting his life back together. My Dad had never talked about that period of time. I realized now I'd never be able to ask him—I'd never be able to find out exactly what happened. I set the thought aside, unable to deal with it.

Suddenly I knew I needed to go by and see the house in Oklahoma City. I knew deeply I must do this. I hadn't been by that house since we left in February of 1967, but strangely enough I knew I would be able to find it—I could just follow the pain it brought up, and the greater the pain, the closer I was. I didn't want to do this on one level, but on another level, I knew it was imperative.

Instead of veering off east to go to Tulsa, I continued north, now on I-35. I drove into Oklahoma City around 3 p.m., just as afternoon traffic was starting to build. I told myself I couldn't stay long, as I would want to avoid rush hour, but part of me knew that was bullshit. I wouldn't stay long because it would hurt so much.

It was easier first to find the school I had attended, and then backtrack to the house, because I could remember the bus route from the school. I left the freeway, drove along 50th Street west and pulled up to Putnam City High School, home of the Pirates. I pulled in to the parking lot, shut down and numb, as a flood of painful feelings tried to rise up, from how unhappy I had been in that building. I knew I must explore and release that pain someday, but today was not the day. I turned around and pulled out heading back east. I saw the intersection that looked like the right one—Vermont Street, and turned onto it, driving north for about a mile. I made a half block jog to the right, and I turned back north. I knew it was the place because I had walked the route from the bus stop and I remembered the daily wondering I felt as I came in sight of the house. Would his car be there? If it wasn't, he had gone to work, a good sign. If it was, he hadn't gone to work, and was home drunk. I pulled to the side of the road where I could see the house sitting on the corner, the front door facing me, the driveway and garage to the left. I hadn't seen that house in

20 years, but I knew—I just knew—that I had left my soul there. It was a feeling that was deep, intense and gut clenching. I was looking at my tomb. I had died in that house, and I didn't know how or why. That instant, sitting in my car, was a life-changing moment, one I had not expected. There had to be a way to find out what went on there, or that deep suicidal death wish that had kicked awake after talking to Wayne would someday conquer me—I just knew it. I put the car in gear, turned the corner and drove on.

Chapter 21

I drove in to Tulsa just after dark, got out of the car and walked into my parent's house. My Mom was really excited to see me, and I was the first of the family to arrive. She had kept some food ready, and we sat right down. After we ate, as we relaxed at the dinner table, she asked how I had been and I told her I was OK. There were some things I needed to ask her about Dad—things I needed to know for my own peace of mind. It was going to be a tough conversation at any time, but it seemed like now might be the time to talk. After the family came in, things would be really hectic, and since I wasn't planning to stay long, we might not get another chance.

"Mother, I need to ask you a couple of things about Dad. Is that too much now? Can you have that talk?"

"Yes, I can talk about Dad. I've been thinking you might have some questions."

"Why is that?"

"Oh, I guess because you were the only son, and fathers and sons is a unique sort of relationship. And since Thanksgiving, a lot of things would have come up." I noticed that she said Thanksgiving, instead of 'since Dad died.'

"So what are you wondering about?" she asked.

"This is kind of tough to get into, but do you ever remember Dad being violent or anything—at the end when we lived in Farmington?"

"No," she said, looking puzzled, "he would mostly give us the silent treatment when he was mad." She thought for a moment. "Why, did he do something to you?"

I didn't think it was of any benefit to replay the incidents in detail—it would just create more pain, so I intuitively kept the details minimal. I just said, "Well, I've had a couple of memories return of when he would hit me." She looked horrified. "You remember in '66 when he and I were arguing over my hair—when I wanted a Beatles haircut?" She nodded. "I think he came into my room late that night and beat me for talking back." I sat and let her absorb that for a moment. "You remember the speech contest in '65 when I was in 9th grade?"

"Sure, I remember. I was terribly proud of all you were doing then."

"I can't remember Dad being there."

"No, he wasn't. He refused to go. For some reason, you doing all that really upset him. Of course, he was drinking more by then, and his job was suffering because of it."

I nodded. "He hit me over that, also, and told me something about not being better than him."

"I could see that being the case. Toward the end he was really sensitive about work—he wasn't doing well at all. And he was struggling about you—you were so quick, and bright, in so many activities and doing so well, that it brought up something in him. It's like it took him back to his junior high days, when he was doing things like that. It almost felt like he was jealous. But I never knew he beat you. Son, I'm so sorry that happened."

"Thanks, Mom. So he never said anything about any of that?"

"Dan, it was about two years ago that we were talking about the end of our time in Farmington. He said that he didn't remember most of '63 to '67. He just didn't know what happened. I honestly think he was blackout drunk many nights during that time."

And there it was—there was my answer, my confirmation. He hadn't been too scared to face what he had done—he just hadn't remembered it.

"What about those four months we were in Oklahoma City? Did he ever talk about that?"

"No, he never said a word. But I think his drinking had progressed to the point that by the time we got to Oklahoma, he was pretty shot—I don't think he would have remembered much."

"OK, then. Well thanks, that helps—it helps a lot. I'm not sure how much you're aware of, but since this stuff has been coming up, it's been kicking me in the ass."

"How do you mean that?"

"Well, a couple of months ago, I had something happen with a guy in Houston, and I was suicidal for a couple of days."

"Yes, I knew about that. Susan told me." I had forgotten talking with my sister about it.

"That's why I need to ask these things about Dad—I'm beginning to uncover some pretty ugly stuff, and it's really deep, and it's got to be dealt with. So thanks for talking with me about it."

"You're welcome, son. Be careful during this time. And let me know what I can do to help."

None of the rest of the family was supposed to arrive that evening, so Mom and I watched TV. I sensed I had talked enough about sensitive issues, and it was time to let it go for a while.

That night as I lay in bed, I reflected on a lot of things. Did it help lessen my anger that my Dad really didn't remember? Yes—and no. Yes, it gave me a sort of peace about my last years with my Dad. We had healed our relationship as far as we could with the ugliness hidden below the surface. He didn't remember—he didn't know those things had happened. As for me—I had just remembered what had happened, but wasn't ready to talk about those events yet, and then he died. It was very unfortunate timing. So that helped me be more at peace that we'd never discussed the poetry, the speech contest, and the hair argument. But did it ease the anger at what had happened? Intuitively I knew it didn't completely clear up my feelings—there was still something unresolved, the anger was still lurking. I didn't care if someone didn't remember or was blackout drunk— what happened to me was horrible, and just not right, damn it!

As soon as I released that thought, another intruded and it may have been the one I was avoiding since I walked in the door of my parent's house. It began to sink in that my Dad wasn't going to be with us this Christmas. Or any holiday. Or ever again. I grew very sad, and lay awake for a long time feeling hollow, before finally drifting off into a restless sleep.

CHAPTER 22

Christmas Eve—which would have been Dad's 60th birthday—was a pretty subdued day. I had slept late, and had a late breakfast with my Mom. Finally around noon my sisters, Nancy and Susan, came in. Susan worked as a nurse in Tulsa—she was a single mother. She brought her young son Justin, age 5. Nancy was married, but her husband wasn't with her. Nancy was a waitress in Stillwater. She brought her young son Fred, the same age as Justin. My third sister, Kitty, lived in Austin, but for some reason hadn't come home for Christmas that year. Of course, Dad was missing. It felt like a pretty small gathering, and it seemed like we were all in some way aware of it. There was an awkwardness as we sat around and visited—everyone was glad to see each other, and wanted to catch up. But it almost felt wrong to feel happy on our Dad's birthday with him so recently gone.

After dinner, we had the traditional Christmas tree and opened presents. It was mostly us sharing in the excitement of presents my Mom had bought for Justin and Fred. That was over fairly quickly, and I sensed things winding down, but I had a final surprise for the family. I had thought for a long time about what I wanted to do with the poem I had written for my Dad. It seemed like a nice tribute to him and I had decided I would like to read it to the family on his birthday, as a gift to them, and as a way to honor my father. I hadn't mentioned it to anyone yet. I thought it would be nice to just go ahead and do it—it wouldn't take long to read, and it would be a quiet way to draw Dad into our gathering.

Everyone was sitting around amid presents and wrapping paper, about to get up and begin to clean up, when I said, "I have one more thing I'd like to do."

The family looked at me, expectantly, a bit puzzled.

"I wrote a poem about Dad, and I'd like to share it with the family." They all nodded and smiled, and I could see Susan and my Mom looking expectantly intrigued. "Would you allow me to read it?"

They all readily agreed, so I went and got the poem, stood before them, and began to read.

"The Ballad of Ben
by Dan Hays

Ben was a treasure,
Gentle and kind.
Men of his stature,
Are so hard to find.

His life went through phases,
Some of them rough.
He walked through each one,
Even when it was tough."

I could sense the room being eerily silent, as if no one was breathing. I could feel myself getting emotional—my chest tightening. I went on.

"In rigorous honesty,
The disease had its way.
Yet he fought it and conquered,
Twenty years day by day.

He cleaned up the wreckage,
Caused by the past.
Returning to living
So freely at last.

He loved his whole family,
Supported us all.
He wanted us happy,
And to walk tall.

With Justin and Fred
He was carefree and happy.
For a gruff old Grand-dad,
He sure acted sappy."

That got a laugh from the family, and I looked up from the paper for the first time. Fred was giggling, Justin was blushing a little, and the tension had broken a bit. I went on.

"His trademark was coveralls,
And plaid tennis shoes."

Another round of giggles. We had all
seen him dressed like that many times, and
could easily bring up the image.

"As on the couch he did lie,
Taking a snooze.

He loved his joking,
'El Supremo' was he,
He got the nickname,
From a madman, you see."

'El Supremo' was the name of a Central
American dictator in a Horatio Hornblower
book, and my Dad had laughingly assigned
himself that label. The ironic joke was that
the dictator was a raving lunatic.

"My dad loved pecan trees,
And working his land.
He gave us an orchard,
With his loving hand.

When he was grafting,
He was at ease.
His time there was special,
Except with the bees."

We all started laughing at that line. Several years ago, my Dad had bought the five
acres with the pecan grove on it. We had all
sensed that some of his happiest moments

were spent out there grafting the pecan trees. Except one time when he accidentally knocked down a hive and got chased by the bees. We were all pretty relaxed after laughing about that incident. I continued.

"Campfires and weenie roasts,
At his special place;
Sharing and laughing,
With joy on his face.

Ben helped many people,
The suffering ones.
He carried the message,
To God's hurting sons."

And suddenly, unexpectedly, I could feel myself choke up as my mind's eye recalled the people who came up after the funeral and told me how my Dad had helped them. I flashed on the man who had said my Dad saved his life. In that moment I had a newer, deeper, clearer awareness of how much he had done with his life. I could feel my shoulders clench as I fought not to break down and cry. It just didn't seem the time or place—it wasn't safe to have feelings that deep here. So I had to just finish. I couldn't look up at the family, or I knew I really would lose it. But I somehow could tell they were struggling like me.

"Sharing and listening,
Whatever it did take;
He gave himself freely,

His spirit awake.

He lived his program,
In all his affairs.
It was an attraction,
For those burdened with cares.

As father and husband
He gave us his best.
We place the memories
In our treasure chest.

He was my father,
I'll shout it out loud,
I loved him dearly,
Of Ben I was proud."

I finished, folded the paper in a room of dead silence, and it seemed like no one was breathing. I glanced up and everyone appeared stunned. Finally, as if out of a reverie, Susan nodded at me, and Mom choked out a quiet thank you. Then everyone quickly got up and began wadding wrapping paper and gathering presents.

We watched TV for the rest of the evening, and no one mentioned the poem again. But I sensed we were all still reflecting on it. I knew I had found out more about my Dad just from reading the poem out loud. I knew now I understood things about him—that helping others was very important to him, and that his work in A.A. was a valuable gift. I just wondered why I couldn't see it before— why I couldn't have sent the poem to him

while he was alive, alive to hear me acknowledge him for his work and say "I'm proud of
you, Dad."

CHAPTER 23

C hristmas Day was very quiet. Nancy had to go back to work, so she and Fred left. Susan also had to work, but Justin stayed with us for the day. We mostly watched TV, each of us inward and somewhat introspective. Mom was quiet, and went and laid down for a nap. It seemed like we needed a respite from all the emotional events that started at Thanksgiving. I could feel a deep pain lingering beneath the surface for me, but it didn't feel like the time or place to let the feelings out, so I went numb and quiet.

Susan came over after work, and we began a crazy quest to eat out on Christmas Day. Mom didn't want to cook and thought we would go to an Italian restaurant that was a favorite of hers and Dad's. It sounded like it had a sentimental attachment for her, so we went along with it. I wondered, though, how many places would be open. We got in the car and drove to the restaurant, only to find it was closed. We spent about an hour driving around Tulsa, trying to find a place to eat, until it began to feel like a compulsive trip. We finally spotted a Chinese buffet that was open and went in and had a Chinese Christmas Day meal.

We went home and sat around for the rest of the evening. My Mom had heard me playing a Frank Sinatra tape that I had made from blending three records, and she really liked it, so I made a copy of it for her. It was a great way to keep my mind occupied.

Late that night as I lay in bed, random thoughts floated to the surface. Memories of returning to Fort Worth, right after the family had split up due to Dad's drinking. Going to the Methodist church my parents had attended when they were young. Meeting a lot of people who were still friends today, and feeling a sense of belonging. I felt like I was home there, and it felt safe.

I became deeply aware of how lucky I was. My life could have gone so many other directions. I could have gone down with the drink, like my Dad had almost done. I knew I carried that potential, but watching him had put a powerful fear of drink in me. I could have killed myself, like what almost happened after talking to Wayne. I didn't know where the thought came from, but I could have ended up in prison. I could have been homeless. I felt sheltered, protected in some way from the demons that haunted me. I felt a yearning and hunger to reconnect with the church. I didn't know if it was to meet a spiritual need, or to try to reclaim the sense of belonging I had felt long ago at the church in Fort Worth. But I felt a need to be connected—somewhere.

Saturday it felt like time to leave. I needed some time to absorb all that had happened. But a massive ice storm had moved in overnight that extended south to Fort Worth, and I didn't want to risk traveling. So I stayed at Mom's and watched TV. It was just the two of us, and we both seemed to need some space, so it was a quiet afternoon. That evening I watched "American Graffiti," and it brought back more memories of high school, particularly about when we moved back to Fort Worth. I finished my junior year in Fort Worth and continued through my senior year at Paschal, the high school my parents had graduated from. I didn't connect with the people in my church until halfway through my senior year, and being new at the school and not knowing people, I stayed at home and was alone most of the time. For some reason, I felt a lot of the feelings of that time coming up—again feeling like the outsider, lonely and needy. My junior year I had spent the first two months in Farmington High School with kids I had known since grade school. Then we moved to Oklahoma City for four months, where I was very unhappy, and suspected something really bad might have happened. Then we moved to Fort Worth, and I was enrolled in Paschal, my third school, to finish the year. By the time I got there, I was pretty introverted, lonely, and unhappy. I felt all of that time bubbling back up as I watched "American Graffiti."

I felt the need to connect so strongly that I called one of the ACA people in Houston, who I knew was having a party that night. It felt like a breath of fresh air to talk to those people, and I stayed on the phone for a while as various people got on to talk to tell me hello. It made me want to cry. I talked with one woman, Vikki, who I had talked with several times before, and found myself pouring out a lot I needed to talk about. I told her about the anger I had been feeling, somehow connected to Dad, but I wasn't sure why. I told her about Mom answering the question—Dad did not remember what happened when I was a teenager. I talked about how I was still short on money, and having to turn it over and trust that it would all work out. She was very sympathetic, understood what I was going through, and supported me in going through the tough emotional journey. I got off the phone feeling reconnected, but it only brought the deep pain closer to the surface. I knew I had to leave as soon as I could to go release the feelings which were bubbling so close to the surface. I thrashed in bed for a long time before settling in to a fitful sleep.

Sunday was better weather in Tulsa, but the ice storm had settled in across north Texas, and it was too risky to go home still. Mom and I talked again in the afternoon, and she gave me a concept which was very foreign to me and left me much to ponder. She said Dad was very proud of my writing. I had never heard of this before. I had given him a draft of a book I had written back in 1985. He had read it, and his only comment was a rather terse, "It was well written." I had thought he was uncomfortable because of the topic, me growing up in an alcoholic home, and he had never said anything more about my writing. But Mom said he was envious of me developing my talent. I didn't know what to think about that and how it fit into everything else I was going through.

I needed a meeting, so Mom took me to where there was an ACA meeting, and she went to the A.A. meeting next door. It felt tremendous to be in the safety of an ACA meeting, and I talked about my Dad's death, and how I was angry and sad, back and forth, in a jumble of feelings.

As I left the meeting, a man came up who must have been at the funeral and recognized me. He told me he knew my Dad from A.A. meetings. Dad seemed very laid back in the meetings and a very neat guy. For some reason, that touched me deeply, and I could feel the feelings bubbling just below the surface. I knew I needed to leave, and I knew I needed to go to Fort Worth—for some reason that felt like a safe place that I needed to reconnect with.

So the next morning, after a hurried goodbye to Mom, I headed back south. It felt like I did so just in time, because the feelings were right on the surface. They were raw and intense, and needed to be released. My father had died, and I needed to grieve.

Chapter 24

I was once asked, "Have you ever felt safe anywhere?" I thought it an interesting question and wondered aloud why it was asked. The person said it was just a feeling they had about me. Wherever it came from, it rang true. I lived with a constant, unformed fear and realized after many years that most situations produced fear in me, and I could not fathom why.

But in answer to the question, I could come up with only one place that truly felt completely safe—my Grandmother Justin's house on Stadium Drive in Fort Worth. I had been visiting that house since I was very young, and it always had a sense of stability for me. I knew that no one could harm me when I was there. I wasn't aware of it until later, but the person I feared was my father. I had several uncles who I saw regularly at that house. I could just sense that my Dad wouldn't try anything around them because they were very proper, powerful men who wouldn't tolerate the sort of things that had gone on inside our house. And my grandmother, Big Mommy, being a very proper

Methodist woman, would never allow anything to get out of line.

My grandmother now lived in a nursing home, but the family had kept her house, so she could occasionally visit—after all, she'd lived there for over fifty years. The family knew the special feeling I had for the house and had agreed I could stay there whenever I visited Fort Worth. It still had all of the furniture in it, and the furnishings were probably all in the same place they had been in when the family first moved there in 1938. It had the feeling of being a sanctuary.

When I was driving back to Houston from Tulsa after Christmas, it was natural to stop over in Fort Worth. With all the feelings that had been stirred up over the holiday, I knew I needed to be in a safe place to let those feelings surface, and the house on Stadium was just the place.

I drove in to Fort Worth Monday, the 28th of December, feeling like I had been shot in the guts, and my insides were wrecked. I felt sad and beyond sad—pain and deeper than pain—to the point I wanted to jump out of my skin. I couldn't sit still and wasn't yet ready to go to Big Mommy's house.

I drove around trying to outrun or escape the pain, which had reached an almost intolerable level—and I had no anesthetic. So I just drove on. I drove by Mathews Memorial Methodist Church—where my parents had gone to church when they were growing up. This was the church I had attended when we moved back to Fort Worth, where I had developed that connectedness and sense of belonging. The building was there, was the same, but felt like a house of ghosts—the people I had known there had all moved on. I could almost envision myself at 17, walking out of the church sanctuary, hurting and bewildered as to why. The vision only deepened my current pain.

I drove by the house on Fuller—where my Mom moved the family to the first house she had ever rented, while trying to raise four children alone. It was the house we were living in when my Dad returned after he had sobered up, to begin living with the family again. I had recently begun to realize that I resented my Mom accepting him back—because I didn't feel completely safe with him around, even now that he was sober. I drove on.

I drove by the houses of Gary and Chip, two friends from the Mathews and high school days. Their parents probably still lived there, but my friends had moved away. I didn't stop.

I drove across town to my other grandmother's house—my Dad's mother, over by Texas Wesleyan College. It was a house with many unpleasant memories—I felt unsafe and unhappy in that house, and had imagined my Dad as a young child living there full-time, and how unpleasant it must have been for him. His Mom was clingy, needy and smothering, and I had begun to suspect, a bit crazy. Her husband had left when my Dad was 11. My first therapist had helped me see that my Dad had turned away from me when I was 11 and that there was a correlation.

All of this flooded back to me as I drove by her house on Hazeline—a small white fronted house with a single car garage, unremarkable from the outside except for the number of memories it revealed to me. I remembered being stuck in her house alone, during the summer when I came to Fort Worth to visit family, while she was at work all day. I remembered having to go out in the hot and humid summer weather to mow her lawn when I came to visit, which didn't feel like much of a vacation. I remembered going down to the drug store to get a cheeseburger and milk shake for lunch—the highlight of my lonely day. I remembered sleeping in the back bedroom of her house, with no air conditioner and the windows and back door open, with only a fan. Feeling sweaty, unsettled and unsafe with the room being so open to the big city, which she had let me know was so very dangerous. I remembered the relief when I could leave her smothering presence to go over to Big Mommy's house, and safety. It seemed like there was a deeper, darker pain locked up inside that house, but I couldn't pin it down. I drove on.

As I drove back across town, I could feel memories of two things. The first was of me—finishing high school in Fort Worth, feeling shell-shocked and wounded and not sure why, deeply sad and unhappy, in spite of my seemingly carefree exterior.

The second flood of memories was about my Dad. My Dad was all about Fort Worth and Fort Worth was all about my Dad. He went all through school in Fort Worth—elementary, junior high, graduating from Paschal High School. He got his college degree at Texas Christian University. He likely accumulated all the pain that led him to drink in Fort Worth. He later sobered up in Fort Worth. I could feel all of it on the surface, and I knew I couldn't go through it alone. I drove up to my grandmother's house, went into the garage, and got the house key. I went inside and turned on a couple of lights, but the safety of her house brought no peace—I was a tightly coiled spring. I called the Al-Anon hotline and found out there was an ACA meeting that night, and knew I had to go. I brought in my luggage, feet like a caged beast as I paced and wandered the house until it was time for the meeting.

I drove out to the meeting location, and the room was locked and darkened. It was time for the meeting to start, and I just intuitively knew there wouldn't be a meeting. I waited fifteen minutes, growing increasingly panicky as my guts hurt more and more deeply. I finally left, meandering around Fort Worth with no destination in sight, needing an escape from the pain and not knowing how to do it. It hurt too deeply to cry, which didn't make any sense to me, but was true.

Finally, in desperation, I pulled up to a bar on the west side of town. I knew this was not a smart choice. I had been struggling over whether or not I was an alcoholic for several years. I had enough episodes of out of control drinking in my past that the answer was right in front of me. But on some deep level I didn't want to be like my Dad—and if I admitted I was an alcoholic, it would be the final, and it felt like fatal, connection to him. So my solution had been to severely curtail my drinking and hope thereby to avoid the admission.

But I rarely, if ever, drank for pleasure—it had always been to avoid pain, like I was doing now. So with great conflict within me outweighed by an even greater need to avoid pain, I went in to the bar and ordered a gin and tonic. And a remarkable thing happened. I had the drink—and I still felt the pain. I knew, of course, that I could continue to drink and blot out the pain. But I also knew from past experience that the anesthetic was only temporary, and should I continue, the next morning I would have a hangover—and still have the pain. It was in that moment of awakening that I knew alcohol would no longer work for me. I reluctantly waved off the bartender's offer of a refill and left, carrying my pain with me. I drove back to my grandmother's house, had a hot shower, lay down in bed, and turned off the lights. I lay there, raw, feeling the pain, for a long time.

Eventually the pain dulled and lessened and I finally drifted off toward sleep, completely tired out and depleted by the whole experience. But as I sank toward sleep, some part of me could appreciate the victory of stepping away from the drink—no, of finding it insufficient as an anesthetic. I knew now it meant I must face the real, deep pain I had avoided for many years, along with the grief over my Dad's death. But I now was very clear that going through that pain was less than the grief I caused myself when drinking too much, waking the next day to find the pain still there and having to go through it all over again. I was ready not to do that any more. Through all the pain, I drifted off to sleep with a tiny smile in the corner of my heart.

Chapter 25

The next day I got up and drove back to Houston, the pain having subsided like a fever breaking. I called Timothy and he wasn't going to have any work for a couple of days. As I sat in my apartment with nothing to do, it gradually dawned on me, by my clenched jaw, knotted stomach and testy attitude, that I was angry. Really angry! Everything that had been going on for the past several months seemed to be a painful time brought on by—God. There, I had said it. This was about God. I was angry at God. That felt like a very fearful place to be—the way some people at the church had presented it, the wrath of God was mighty and much to be feared. It was alright for God to be angry, but not men. It was especially bad to be angry at God. But there I was. I somehow knew that this anger was an essential part of what I was going through, and it needed to be released, fearful though that process might be.

I knew I needed to write it all down as a personal inventory. This was baggage I was carrying around with me, it was a liability I needed to deal with, and the writing process was the way to face up to it. I had done it before, and I trusted that this process would work. I knew I had to own the anger and see the anger for what it was, to break my denial about it, and to see what it was about, in order to begin to release it. I began to write.

> *My anger at Dad, God and the church*
>
> *For several years I have been unable to feel the anger at my Dad for how he abused me when I was a child. The payoff from not getting angry at Dad was to avoid the possibility of abuse, physical and emotional, and the terror it brought up. So I would redirect my anger at Dad toward anything or anyone else. Not out of respect for him, but out of fear. I was so terrified of the man, after the incident at 16. When I stood up and argued with him, and he came into my room late at night and beat me. I deserve to get angry. I have a right to get angry. He abused me every way possible. He robbed me of my self, my creativity, all parts of me. No one deserves that. I deserve to be angry.*
>
> *I'm angry because my Dad was a coward who never had the courage to face up to what he did to me—directly. He made indirect amends but never admitted that he had harmed me, never owned up to "the wreckage of the past." And I've been letting him off*

the hook saying he was blacked out. I don't know that. He may have remembered everything. He cheated me out of the reality of it.

Anger at God.

I am furious (Danny talking) at God, because I trusted and believed in Him, and He allowed all the crap that happened. Where were You, God, when my Dad was beating me? You abandoned me, and let him kill me—a soul death. I hate You, God. I can't trust You. You went away when I needed You most.

Then You let my Daddy die. Why? If I trust You, will you do something like that again? The evidence says no, but I can't get past this. I'm stuck, and that's just where I am. I feel like You hate me and are trying to kill me, because Daddy beats me and I don't deserve to live.

Payoff from anger:

My anger bonds me to others—by hate. I, Danny, use my anger to keep people away from me. Because of my shame, which says I don't deserve love. And because if I keep people away, they can't hurt me. But my anger is a cancer which killed my Dad, and which is poisoning me.

The payoff from my anger—it protects me from the hurt and sadness. Sadness that this disease caused Daddy to beat me. Sadness and hurt that I did not feel lovable or worthwhile. It blocks forgiveness and acceptance. My anger at God is a block which keeps me from trusting Him. It screws up my whole life.

Payoff—it gives me an excuse not to trust God, to blame Him for things that happen, and not take responsibility for my life. It only hurts me. But I am powerless over my anger, and have to trust God to remove it.

But damn it, God, You didn't remove Daddy's anger and it killed him. So what about that, Big Fella? If you are true and faithful, why did You let Daddy down? Why are You giving me this choice? I really have felt like You wanted me to die. I'm beginning to believe You don't. But Daddy never lost that death wish. (His smoking after all his health issues seemed like slow suicide.) So why do I get to walk past this, God? I don't understand. I'm pissed. It isn't fair.

Shame keeps me from getting angry. Anger keeps me from feeling shame. It's a vicious cycle, and it pisses me off. I once again cut the cord to Daddy's shame. I'm angry that I had to carry his shame. I don't like any of this. My Daddy's gone and I can't spend time with him. We were just getting to know each other.

Also, God, I'm angry at Your church for the crap they taught me.

About the angry, punishing God. About rigidity, narrow-mindedness, false superiority, about the tools of fear, guilt and shame that the church uses. I spit that crap out, God. I want to see You as loving. But I am powerless.

Why do You allow alcoholism? The disease makes me hate the ones I love. I'm angry about that. God, teach me a new way to see You.

Love,
Dan

Those thoughts had all come out in such a rush that I knew they had been bottled up for a long time. I got up, went out on the back porch, and stood looking out at the back yard. I was aware that by writing those words, I had revealed a cancer within me that had been festering for a long time. I knew that in saying I was angry at God, I had opened up a whole new area, a whole new—rebellion? Possibly rebellion, but possibly a whole new level of healing, because for the first time I had really been honest about my feelings toward God. It somehow felt like God was chuckling. He had known all along that poison was there, and had pushed me into a corner to reveal and feel them. Interesting thought, and the way I was recently, I wondered if any of it was true, or just another fantasy of an overstressed and tortured mind. I shuddered for a moment, and walked back inside.

Chapter 26

The next day I just let the impact of the words I had written sink in. It still bothered me that Wayne had tried to rob my writing from me. When I had been at the early stages of trying out my path as a writer, Wayne had supported it. Yet when it became more real, he slapped it back down. He showed almost dismay that I was more actively pursuing my writing, and then he threw out the slap—"*at this point, your writing is a fantasy.*" That still rankled me. I began to make connections. It was like what had happened with my Dad when I was 14. I published the poems in the literary magazine, tried to tell him about it to share my joy, and he put down my writing—he robbed my joy and my dream. Aha!

Through making that connection, I began to see how strong had been my need to win the approval of a certain type of man, an authority figure man. How tenuous was my belief that I could win that approval. How easily my dreams could be crushed by their seeds of doubt—the ground had been sown for those doubts early, and I wasn't free to feel the joy of my creativity.

I had a glimpse of some thoughts that I couldn't quite pull together but which I knew were significant. The last year before my Dad died he had been much more supportive of me, my dreams, and my way of life, which was a contradiction to the way he had abused me as a child. Could it be I went to Wayne because I needed some of the old abuse and knew on some level he would respond like he did? Honestly, there were others I could have gone to for support—why had I chosen Wayne? Was I seeking the familiar? I made a mental note to explore that thought further, and then I set it aside for the moment.

For now I knew that the writing I had done yesterday, though brief, was very important. I knew I must make it more real—acknowledge the depth of that anger to myself and to God. Suddenly I knew I must also read it aloud to someone—someone I trusted, but also someone who represented that which I was angry at—an agent of God and the church, if you will. A minister. Tom, the youth minister at our church, was one candidate for reading my thoughts with, but for some reason it didn't feel right to do it with him; we were too close. I sensed I needed someone more distant, able to be objective to what I was saying. Suddenly, I knew who it would be. There was a minister at our church I liked very much—Ronald Townsend. I had met him through Tom, who respected him greatly, and I instinctively thought a lot of Ronald and felt comfortable with him. I trusted him—I knew I would have to trust a minister a lot to read what I had written, because I wasn't strong enough to risk another put-down like I had gotten from Wayne. I knew I would be safe with Ronald.

I called the church and was put through to him. He answered the phone.

"Ronald, this is Dan Hays."

"Hey, Dan, how are you doing? I heard about your Dad, I'm sorry to hear about that."

"Thank you, Ronald. I appreciate that. I'm doing pretty well, considering."

"I understand. To what do I owe the pleasure of this call?"

"Ronald, I was wondering if you would have some time where we could sit and talk? My Dad's death has brought up some things I need to talk through."

"Sure. Let me look at my calendar. How does tomorrow at 2:00 p.m. sound?"

"Ronald, that sounds wonderful. Thanks. But I just want to be up front—I want to read to you something I've written—and it's about some anger at God and the church. Would that make you uncomfortable to hear that?"

He chuckled. "Not at all, Dan. It wouldn't be the first time I've heard something like that—or said something like that. Bring what you've got, and we'll go through it."

"Thanks, Ronald, I will. I'll see you to-morrow."

"Two p.m. it is. I'll see you then. Looking forward to it."

"Goodbye."

Though I felt some anxiety after I hung up at having committed to do this, from Ronald's responses, I felt safe and knew things would be alright.

———————

Of course I didn't sleep soundly that night, and I was pretty anxious by the time I pulled up to the church the next day. Yet I knew I must do this—it was part of my healing. It would make the anger real, help me get to it where I could begin to release it.

I went in to the church offices, Ronald came out and shook my hand, and we went into his office and closed the door. He asked me again how I was doing, and we chatted for a few moments. Then he got down to it.

"So, you've got something you need to let out, huh?"

I nodded.

"How would you like to do it? Do you want to go through it a bit at a time and have me give you feedback, or would you just like to read what you've written straight through?"

"Ron, I think I'd just like to read it all— it's not very long, and then we can talk about it."

He nodded and leaned forward against his desk, elbows on the desk, fingers intertwined, an open and genuine look on his face. "OK, I'm ready if you'd like to read."

I began. "I am angry at God." I looked over at him, and he was nodding, agreeing with my sentiment. I read about my anger at God, my anger at the church, my anger at the muddled messages of the Bible teachers. I read about God allowing my Dad to abuse me and not stopping it. I read about being angry at my Dad and how he abused me. I tried to read the words slowly and carefully, trying to feel each word as it rolled from my tongue, to realize the weight and gravity of my words. I read of my disgust (wow, that felt strong) with the God—church—authority figure—Dad thread of my life. I could feel myself getting the power of my words on a whole new, very visceral way. I finished, scarcely breathing. I knew this was a big moment.

Ron looked at me, then he said the most amazing words. "You know, if God is who most people say He is, He's a prick."

I was stunned, and just nodded in mute agreement. He got it! He understood. He didn't put down my feelings. I felt vindicated. I felt supported.

"Dan, I think what you've read is thoughts that are shared by a lot of people. You just don't hear them much around church because most people are too afraid to verbalize them—afraid of potential ostracism. But I agree with you that God is portrayed in some pretty skewed ways by the church—well, by some Bible teachers."

I just nodded at him.

"Dan, I really like the way you ended what you wrote. 'God, teach me a new way to see You.' He will do that. By you honestly telling Him you're angry with Him, you've opened the lines of communication in a whole new way. And God will honor that. But don't be surprised if things continue to be revealed to you. It sounds like some pretty ugly things happened to you as a child. Things like that tend to fester like an open wound and have to be drained off to heal. What you have done today will only help that process. It took great courage to do what you did today."

It was like he could sense I had gone as far as I could, because he then suggested we pray together. He offered a brief prayer for my insight, healing, and releasing old pains. Then we stood, he shook my hand with a warm smile on his face, wished me well, and I left. I walked out of the church offices to the parking lot in somewhat of a daze. I almost felt numb, but different—in what way I could not tell. But I knew I had initiated something—some process I did not yet fully understand. But I suspected Ron was right—today might lead to further insights. Little did I imagine how true that would be.

Chapter 27

After a couple of days of not working, it began to sink in that I was probably out of a job. I began to realize, the way Timothy had talked, it wasn't a temporary shortage of work, but that he no longer had any need for help. Which left me with a lot of time on my hands—time to reflect on the words I had read aloud to Ron, time to reflect on and feel my anger. Yet underneath that, I could feel fear—no, not fear—terror. I wasn't sure what the terror was about, but it seemed to be about jobs. The thought of going to look for another job terrified me, and I felt paralyzed about it, and unable to act, which frustrated me. I felt like I was fighting against something God would not reveal to me, and somehow I was supposed to guess what it was.

Finally, it all boiled over. I had gone to a noon ACA meeting out at Holy Name Retreat Center, and I felt my anger, frustration and fear blending into a steely blue rage. I went out behind the retreat center into a large wooded area. I began to yell at God, "Damn it, God, where are You? What's going on with me? Am I some kind of puppet You are playing with?" I let out a scream, as loud and long as I could, from deep down in my gut. Then I yelled, "Damn it, Dad, I can't believe what you did to me. This is what got me hurt as a kid—when I talked back to you, you beat me. You coward! How could you do that? And Wayne—you did the same thing—you got me at a time when I was down and vulnerable, and you kicked me with your slick bullshit words. 'I've been where you are, Dan.' Sure, Wayne, I'm supposed to believe you've really ever gone through what I have been experiencing? Give me a break, you silver spoon rich boy. Don't even think I'm buying that."

Finally, I began to wind down, and I sat on a bench feeling spent. I talked out loud some more with God, now that I had calmed down.

"Dear God, what the heck is going on? It feels like I'm missing something and I can't tell what it is. I don't feel a sense of Your presence. It feels like when my Dad was beating me—and You were nowhere to be found. What's that all about? I know I need to find some more work, but the thought of even looking terrifies me. Why? Why is this job thing such a big issue? I mean, Wayne saying 'Just go out and get a job' sounds like the right thing to do, and so very obvious. It would be easy for him, and I truly felt he didn't understand or hear what I had been trying to say to him—that it's not that easy for me. I couldn't figure out how to say that,

God, and not feel silly, because I don't know why getting a job terrifies me."

I looked up at the sky and another long scream welled up from deep within me, and I knew it was directed at God. I knew He knew it, too. I sat with that awareness for a while longer and then drove home. As I drove, I suddenly realized part of why I was angry with Wayne—because for so long I had wanted to be like him—the successful businessman, the Bible teacher, the charismatic leader, the authority figure everyone looked to for guidance, the man with the final word—which was about Dad, also—the person with the ability to control my life. But I couldn't have handled being that person—it was too much about ego and self-centeredness, and I would have gone overboard with the power. Somehow, I realized that whatever I was going through, it was giving me the humility not to become the way Dad had acted when he was drunk. I was getting the humility of being completely powerless to conquer the demons which assailed me and, therefore, having to rely on God—even as I was mad at Him.

That evening the fear hit. Fear because I had told Ronald I was mad at God, that I had yelled out loud at God. What if the punishing God was true? I was now vulnerable. I could get hurt like my Dad had hurt me. I had never gone out on a limb like this before in expressing anger at God. Even though Ronald had supported it—he wasn't the one who had expressed anger at God. I just felt exposed and insecure about what I had done and what it might lead to.

And underneath there was the terror. I needed a job. I needed to go find a job. I was frozen at the thought of looking for a job. I felt the terror come up, pushed it back down and submerged it again. I finally went to bed and fell into a fitful sleep, having dark and disturbing dreams I could not remember when I awoke the next morning.

CHAPTER 28

T he next night I went to see a movie with some friends. I needed a break from all the emotional turmoil swirling around in me. I didn't get that break. I went with two women from the ACA program, and someone suggested the movie "Suspect" starring Cher and Liam Neeson. It sounded like a sort of light detective movie, yet it turned out to be one of the scariest movies I'd ever seen. It seemed to magnify and amplify the fear I was feeling. It was about a lawyer, played by Cher, trying to solve a murder, and one of the critical witnesses was a mute, homeless person, played by Liam Neeson. There was one scary scene early in the movie where someone sprang out of the dark, all three of us jumped, and one of the women screamed and grabbed my arm, scaring me even more. I never relaxed for the rest of the movie. It was really intense.

One of the characters from the movie disturbed me deeply. He was a homeless person named Michael, obviously deranged. Yet he kept spouting off religious sayings as if he had all the answers. He seemed discon- nected from reality. It started thoughts I didn't want to pursue, tried to push away. Thoughts about me, about my current situation. What if I was just like that guy? I didn't want to go there, but the images of that crazy homeless guy kept floating around the edges of my consciousness, like fireflies.

After we left the movie, as we stood out in the parking lot talking, I could feel myself being in an "on patrol" mentality—would be the best I could explain it—my threat detectors were on high alert for any enemies hiding in the shadows around the parking lot. I was alert to changes and nuances in my environment, hyper-sensitive to any movement, ready to bolt and run—or stand and fight—at any moment, depending on the danger. I could feel my heart pumping, electricity in my veins; I was supercharged. I somehow knew this emotional state was not all from the movie, but something else, only freed up by seeing the movie. I had the sense that someone was coming after me and that they were getting closer.

We said our goodbyes and I drove home, feeling almost as if I were somewhere else. As I parked, got out and walked into my apartment, I felt myself being back in Farmington in that house on Crescent Street, age 16 or so, dark wintry, cold night like it was outside right now, late at night. I was frozen in bed, thinking I heard footsteps approaching from somewhere outside my room, but unable to cry out for help. Terrified, shadows, fears. Afraid he would come in and get me. It never occurred to me to ask for help.

Afraid—of God—expecting Him to punish me. After all, I had spoken up. I had talked back to God. I had expressed anger at God—in front of one of his own people. I was in fear for my life. But to ask for help for some reason brought up terror. I was somehow weak if I asked—if I pointed to the real issue—he would kill me. Going for job interviews—interviewers—authority figures—brought up terror. Someone having great power over me—brought up great terror. Like Wayne had power over me. Now—I had no money. I had no job. I felt trapped, frozen, unable to move. I had to trust God and ask for help. Just having the thought brought up greater terror. What if God wasn't who I thought? What if He was not there? Or had deceived me? Terror! Powerless, yet in some way, aware. Knowing something deep was trying to push to the surface.

When I awoke the next morning, I lay in bed, too frightened to get up. I realized that I had been at this point many times before. I couldn't reach out. I couldn't take the next step—I couldn't ask for help. I couldn't move. I had seen so many jobs fall through. So many failures that made no sense. I felt beyond a terror—it was like a numbness—total body numbness, unable to move. I could see how that sensation had occurred many times through my life. Being a real estate salesman in Austin—spending time scouting the market and looking at houses, but being scared to actually meet and work with a customer.

Over the years I had made many prepa-
rations to get jobs but had relatively few interviews. Why was that? But I realized this
happened only when I was pursuing "success" jobs. Early in 1986 I had interviewed
with a sales manager. The conversation had
drifted to my Dad being a salesman. The
man commented, "You have a really strong
success pattern in your career. You have far
exceeded what your Dad accomplished." The
comment brought up a lot of indefinable and
disturbing feelings. I pushed away his comment like I had pushed away the comments
about me being a poet and a good public
speaker. It was the same sort of feeling—
don't let that be true—it's a dangerous truth.

I had always run from the hideous feeling I was having now when it came time to go
out and find a job. But I realized I was at a
crossroads—either keep running from the
feelings, or begin facing the terror—however
horrifying that thought might be. I decided
just to stay with the feelings. No, that wasn't
accurate—that implied choice. I couldn't
move—couldn't begin the movement to get
out of bed. Frozen. I didn't know what the
terror was about or where it came from. I
thought I had worked through being paralyzed with fear. Yet here it was, in full force,
cementing me to my bed.

I thought of the movie "Suspect"; Michael, the crazy street person, spouting religious talk. He was my nightmare—that I was
so damaged I was crazy—not on a walk of
faith. I knew I was powerless, but unable to

reach out to God and allow Him to help me. I felt stuck, trapped, and unable to move.

Wayne and his "get out and get a job" stuff. He appeared to have no experience of the damage I'd suffered, didn't know how emotionally loaded that direction was for me. He either didn't see or ignored that something deeper was going on. That sort of thing would be easy for him—someone who could just charge through obstacles toward success. I was frustrated—feeling rage rumbling below the surface—rage born from living a long time in terror, coupled with feeling trapped, like I was trapped in the house with Dad in the dead of winter.

God, are You there? I am in the garden, and I am dying. What's going on? What happened to me? I had to hang on to the hope of "Hind's Feet on High Places", one of my favorite books. It was about a woman named Much Afraid who lived in the Valley of Fears and started on a journey to the high places. I clung to the hopeful message of that book, that the woman was given the strength to confront and overcome her fears. I had forgotten how I used to lay in the bed with the covers over my head—paralyzed with fear and unable to move. I was back at that old familiar place. I felt hopeless. It was all over. I knew I had run the race as far as I could. I couldn't go any further. I felt crippled, lame and weak. I was Much Afraid—unable to reach High Places; unable to free myself, yet surrendered to the pain. I would die rather than ask for help. I sensed such terrible damage. Why?

Yet somehow, I was not panicky. Always before I had panicked and run from this place. I felt calm—in one sense. Almost as if I didn't care anymore. Who cares if they repossessed my car? If I didn't eat? If I ended up a street person? What if God had deceived me? Abandoned me?

God, provide me a miracle. Help me. Yet I was so different than I once was. If it all stopped here, I had come farther than I thought possible. I had received love. I had despaired of that.

I lay there a while longer and then the paralysis subsided for the moment, and I got up to go eat breakfast.

CHAPTER 29

The next day I went to a noon ACA meeting at Holy Name Retreat Center. A lot of people were out of work or having trouble finding jobs because the oil industry had crashed, leaving a lot of us caught without work. So work and jobs came up once again as a topic. I felt myself start shaking during the meeting, not sure why, but too terrified to speak up. After the meeting, I went out behind the center into the glade where I had yelled at God, too afraid to go home and be alone, wanting to be in a safe place, and Holy Name felt as safe as I could get. It was a warm afternoon, mid 60s outside, so I sat on a bench, felt the hush of the breeze through the tall pine trees, felt the warmth of the sun.

Suddenly things began to come into focus. My fears had something to do with jobs; I knew that much. But more than that—getting a successful job was the point of fear. I started to connect things—I went back through things that I had realized before, but I began to see a pattern. When I was going through college—the group of us working on the maintenance crew for a group of food stores in Fort Worth. After several summers my friends began to move on to summer intern-type jobs to better prepare themselves for career jobs. Yet, I stayed at that job—stuck, unhappy, yet almost feeling incapable of seeking anything better.

Then when I was finishing college and it was time to start interviewing for jobs, I suddenly decide to go into graduate school, which postponed the job search question. In graduate school, I dropped out because I was broke and worked in the oilfields to earn money to finish school. Somehow the oilfield job hadn't brought up any fear.

Then when graduate school was almost over, I began interviewing, but I would walk away from interviews feeling I hadn't given my best. I hadn't acted like I really wanted the job.

A friend's dad helped me get a job at an oil company, so I had work, but I was aware I wasn't really utilizing my graduate degree, and yet had trouble looking for a more suitable fit. I would know it was time to advance my career, but I hesitated to begin.

Finally, I had the interview in Dallas for a position I really wanted. A successful job in a career field—petroleum landman—I really wanted to be in. I went to lunch with the interviewer and another prospective employee, and froze up. I showed no personality, no initiative, nothing to make me appealing and a candidate for that job. I didn't get the job.

I didn't get the job—it seemed to be a refrain from my career and the pattern came into focus—me avoiding "success," success being a fearful—no, terrifying—prospect.

What happened? Where was I? I could feel sensations returning, almost a feeling memory returning. I could feel it coming. Dad got promoted or something—and we moved from Farmington to Oklahoma City. I got my first job. There was a threat of him losing his job. Was there a comment? Was I shaming Dad to have a job when he was about to lose his? Was that what this was about?

"Don't you ever think you're better than me. Just because you're working, do you think you're better than me?" The words were suddenly there, and I could hear them clearly said in my Dad's voice. I wasn't sure where or when the words were said, but I knew—I now knew clearly that those words or something similar had been said to me. I suddenly remembered how I had been compelled to go by the house in Oklahoma City on my way to Tulsa. The house I had not seen in 20 years. Just like that I knew those words had been said inside that house. At about this time of year. In January, when it was cold, bitter cold, in the dark of night. I shuddered, in spite of the warm sun on my back.

I got out a small notebook I carried with me to write things down as I thought of them. I began to write.

My deepest fears:
1) That God has deceived me.
2) That God will abandon me.

3) That I am not on a spiritual path but actually crazy.

4) That I am congenitally incapable of coping with life.

5) That I will end up as a psycho street person.

The vision of the homeless person, Michael, in the movie "Suspect" kept floating past my vision. What if this entire job thing was some delusional process of my clouded mind? What if my vision of writing was the same? What if Wayne was right and it was just as simple as going out and getting a job. I couldn't tell. I did know that jobs felt like a double bind. I was compelled to get a successful business job, to make my Dad proud of me. Yet I was also compelled not to exceed him, so not to shame him. So I would sabotage success jobs. By not looking. By screwing up the interview. It all floated around in my mind turbulently, and I couldn't sort out truth from fiction, truth from delusion. But I knew I was desperate and willing to do anything to figure this mess out.

———

The next day I was sitting in my apartment when my direction came to me. I knew there was a part of me that was still a scared little boy. I had named him "Little Danny." He was my inner child—a buzz phrase at the time, but it seemed to fit. When I thought of that part of me, I could visualize about a 14-

year-old boy, sitting in his room, terrified, a tear running down his cheek, wondering why his daddy would hurt him. He was terrified, gifted, talented, sensitive and caring, yet highly puzzled by the events of his world. I was also aware that this part of me was a very spiritual connection to God, was the seat of my intuition, and he knew what had happened to me—to him—as a child. But he was terrified to speak of it.

My ACA sponsor had stretched me several times by telling me about Gestalt exercises. He would suggest that I set up two chairs facing each other, sit in one, and speak to another person—Mom, Dad, whoever—that I needed to clear the air with. Then he would have me switch chairs and speak from the perspective of the other person. It sounded pretty hokey when he told me about it, but a therapist I had gone to had also mentioned the same concept, so I guessed there was some validity to it. I had tried it by myself at home a couple of times, and it seemed to bring some relief. My sponsor had suggested also using that technique with my inner child, but there had been some resistance to actually sitting down and doing it, so I hadn't tried.

Yet, I sensed that this was the time, and I was willing to try anything. If it didn't work—what had I lost? What exactly was the risk? A few minutes in sitting in a chair feeling silly? It was worth it for the chance that it might do some good.

It only felt safe enough to do this in my apartment, during daylight. So I set two chairs in my living room facing each other.

I sat in one, and as Dan, began to speak.

"Danny, are you there? Are you willing to listen to me?"

It felt really goofy, and I was glad I was alone, but I kept on. I could sense something happening, but wasn't sure exactly what.

"Danny, I know you're scared. Are you scared?"

Suddenly I felt compelled to get up and switch chairs. As I sat in the other chair, I felt different.

"Yes, I'm really scared. I'm terrified."

I was shocked to hear how my voice changed; it was high-pitched and tight. It was the voice of a terrified young boy. I switched chairs again.

"Danny, I understand. I know you're terrified. But Danny, I'd like to ask that you trust me. I won't let you get hurt again. And if we're going to get past this, I'd like for you to consider telling me what happened. Would you do that? I get the feeling you know what happened. It was in Oklahoma City, wasn't it?"

I switched chairs again. "Yes, it was there. It was late at night." I could feel my voice quivering. "I came in late, about 1 a.m., from my job at the burger joint. I was really proud of that job." It all came back; the sights and smells of that first job, clatter of dishes, sizzle of cooking burgers, babble of conversations, clearing tables, washing dishes, the exhilaration of doing my job well, of getting a paycheck, of feeling a bit independent, of feeling very proud of what I was doing.

"I walked in the house, and usually everyone was already asleep. But that night Dad was still awake. I said I'd been at my job. He got real angry with me and beat me up after I mentioned my job. I was bloody." I could feel my face twitching. "He was angry because I had a job. He said 'don't think you're better than me because you have a job.' " And Danny stopped talking.

I got up and sat in the other chair. I thanked Danny for telling me what had happened, and I told him he had done really well. As I sat there I remembered more of what had happened. The next morning, my face had been bruised, and I knew I couldn't go to school, so I stayed home. Somehow, I also knew I couldn't ask for help. If I did, someone would find out about Dad, and he would get angry and beat me worse. So I was trapped. Dad had been home a lot during that time—mostly drunk—and was probably about to lose his job. Mom was sick a lot and may have been in the hospital for what they called the nervous breakdown.

The message was: if you have a job, you shame Dad. If you have a successful job, you can get hurt. Jobs brought up TERROR. Of being killed.

Killed?? Where did that come from?

Chapter 30

The next several days, I was in shock as the magnitude of what Little Danny had revealed to me began to sink in. Then one night I had a dream.

I was sitting on top of a hill with a shotgun. I was stalking someone below me. I had to defend myself or the person would kill me. Suddenly I knew the person had cut me off from where my ammo was stashed down below, and the person was coming after me. I was out of ammo. I ran back up the hill, and knew he was coming after me with a high powered rifle. I ran into a deserted mine shaft, and I kept getting blocked by boards in my way. I heard him right behind me and knew he was about to fire. I turned to look, and it was my Dad. I woke up, clammy and terrified, my breath shallow and rapid.

———

The next night I dreamed again. I had taken over my Dad's job and his responsibilities. I was in some place far away from home—unfamiliar. It was grey and cold and dead. I had his house; I lived in his house.

Then I was in his office and was expected to do his job. Sales—oilfield services. They were pushing me to call on his customers. To keep up his reputation. I felt helpless and trapped, I felt doomed. I felt lost—unable to perform his functions. Unwilling. Resistant. Yet powerless—at the behest of forces of authority. I had no choice, and I had to do this job. I felt hopeless, dead. I was in his office, reminiscent of Dad's office in Tulsa. Many stories off the ground. Unable to get away, unsure of what to do next. I knew if I continued this path it would suck the life out of me and I would die. I was hesitant. I wanted to sell his house, quit his job and leave, yet I was somehow unable to do so. I felt obligated to stay—it was my duty as his son. I felt guilty for feeling unwilling. I felt despairing and unable to see why I felt so trapped.

I awake from that dream sensing that it told me a lot, but I couldn't see it—the feeling of being trapped was too intense to clearly see anything else.

Chapter 31

About four days after I had the dreams, I
felt a need to be moving. A lot of jumbled thoughts were floating around in my
head and I couldn't pull them apart. Sometimes exercise helped me think things
through. Only it was rainy and cold outside.
So I decided to go mall-walking. I still wasn't
working, and I had plenty of time in the middle of the afternoon. It was a weekday, so I
knew the mall wouldn't be overly crowded. I
got in the car and drove over to the Galleria.
It was a large three-level mall on the west
side of Houston, and I'd gone walking there
before. There were wide walkways and since
it was such a large mall, long stretches for
walking. An ice rink sat in the middle of the
bottom level, a good place to pause and
watch skaters. There was a nice sense of
anonymity about blending in with shoppers,
enough motion to occupy the mind navigat-
ing around people and plenty of window
shopping opportunities. But as I parked and
walked into the mall, I knew I'd stop and
spend some time at the pet store—watching
the various animals in their cages. I found
the parakeets and parrots especially fasci-

nating. I decided I'd walk off some energy first and save the pet store as a treat at the end.

I rode escalators up to the third floor and began to walk. I reflected on something which had happened a couple of days ago. A friend had told me about a man who did personality testing to help people pick careers and find jobs. Of course I couldn't afford that right then, but it turned out the guy was a retired engineer, Joseph Black, who did testing because he liked it and would do it for free. I had gone over to the man's house and taken his tests, and he had given me an evaluation, which he had taped for me to listen to later.

I stopped and looked at some shirts in a men's store then walked on—it felt like looking at a candy store when you're too broke to buy, so I quickly moved on.

One thing the man had done really struck me. He was talking about how I had a lot of integrity. To illustrate that, he took out his wallet, placed it on my side of the table, right in front of me.

"I would feel very comfortable," he had said, "giving you my wallet. I am completely certain that if you were to keep it for me for several days, I would get it back with everything in it."

I had nodded in agreement, because I understood what he was saying and knew it to be true. Now, through the crowd noises and faint sounds of blades on ice from below, the import of the symbolic gesture sank in for me. He had highlighted the incongruity of Wayne's comments that reflected on my character and integrity. "You've stiffed your creditors." I could hear the words again is if he had just said them with that almost sarcastic overtone in his voice. He had made it sound like I had intentionally and willfully set out to harm those I owed money. I didn't feel angry right then, but it stood out more clearly what a falsehood Wayne had tried to lay on me. It puzzled me. Why would he do that? It bothered me, and I had not found an answer for it. I stopped and leaned against the rail, watching the skaters two floors below.

Somehow, I knew that Joseph Black had given me a real gift with the gesture with his wallet. He gave me back something Wayne had tried to take away. I had the symbolic gift of the wallet to restore some of my sense of my integrity—that I had been doubting since my talk with Wayne.

I had considered the evaluation as a sort of present to myself—my birthday, January 18th, had come and gone quietly as usual, because I never wanted any fuss made over it. The few times my friends had tried to do something for me, they had to make it a surprise party—I guess they could tell I might not show up if I knew what they were planning. I had known I was like that for years and had occasionally wondered why that aversion was so strong. But at least now it was over for another year. Then I had the thought—I had gone to my first ACA meeting on my actual birthday. I remember being in a lot of pain that night. Why would that special day be so painful?

January—my birthday—cold, dark night. Somehow the thoughts started to connect as I walked on, occasionally slowing or side-stepping to avoid shoppers. I wondered if any of them were trying to put together pieces of their past—to remember. I knew it had something to do with the time we lived in Oklahoma City. I had been so strongly drawn to drive by the house where we lived in Oklahoma City, the one where I could feel darkness and pain. Even now, the mall walking felt reminiscent of Oklahoma City. I used to go walk at Penn Square Mall, enjoying the temporary anonymity, the feeling of invisibility, the feeling of safety while no one knew where I was.

My Dad had been transferred to Oklahoma City—or had he asked for a transfer? I knew he was drinking more. He was staying home from work. Was he about to lose his job? Was Mom around? It seemed like she had gone in the hospital in December of 1966, but by January, she would have been back home. Late in December I got the job as a busboy at the hamburger place. I remember I was working late hours there. I knew that because I was so tired I fell asleep in Algebra class several times. I was tired a lot, but I think being out of the house made it worth the lack of sleep. So I would have walked into the house, late at night, and would have expected him to be passed out.

But one night he wasn't. He hit me, I think, until I was bloody, and then made that comment, "Don't think you're better than me because you've got a job." I felt my breath catch, and I walked faster.

As I walked, I suddenly began humming a tune. The words started coming to me. A song from the '60's I'd heard recently on the radio. "For What It's Worth," by the Buffalo Springfield. It had haunted me ever since it first came out—omigosh, early in 1967! I bet it was playing while we were living in Oklahoma City. I kept singing the song in my head, the significance of the words suddenly new, alive and scary, dangerous. I stopped, my feet stuck to the floor like lead.

"There's something happening here,
what it is ain't exactly clear.
There's a man with a gun over there,
telling me I got to beware."

The song played on in my head, as I tried to absorb the meaning and impact of the words.

"Paranoia strikes deep,
into your life it will creep,
Starts when you're always afraid,
Step out of line,
The man come and take you away."

I saw a woman glance at me with an odd, alarmed look, and I knew I must have some kind of strange, horrified look on my face. I quickly began walking. That song had haunted me since the 60's, but I had always assumed it was just because it was an intense, dark sort of ballad. But now I knew—I could get it on a whole new level—there was more. I thought of the dream—a man chasing me with a gun, I turned and looked and the man was my Dad, and he was about to kill me. As I walked, I could feel a spot in the middle of my back. It was dead center between my shoulder blades, and was about the size of dime—or a bullet hole. My back tensed up, expecting the sound of a shot, the impact pushing me forward. It felt so vivid I couldn't believe it. I stopped walking and sat down on a bench to catch my breath.

Winter—January 1967—Dad at home—me coming in from my job—him mad about it—and? I knew there was more. I could tell there was more. I didn't know what—for sure. But I could guess—even though I didn't really want to. Suddenly I'd had enough of mall walking and quickly went back out to the car, pulled out of the parking lot and drove off. I could tell I was about to remember more of what had happened back then. I knew I would have to feel really safe to let that memory surface. What would make me feel that safe? I knew I had come to a crossroads—if I now ran from what was trying to surface, I would have to keep avoiding it, and running from it—and I would never be free to stop running. Facing it would be scary, but I knew I had to, and soon. With that awareness, I began to breathe a little more easily, because however painful it might be, I was going to face the mysterious force which had so strongly skewered my reality for many years. As I pulled into the driveway at home, I knew I was pretty shaken up, because I had left the mall without even visiting the pet store and seeing the parakeets. I had completely forgotten.

Chapter 32

For the next several days, I think I just wandered around a lot in a daze—or in shock. I knew now that there was more to remember about what had happened in Oklahoma City. I wasn't terribly thrilled at the idea of remembering. Yet I knew I had to—it seemed like that moment was the key which would unlock these puzzling events of my life. But I knew I couldn't do it alone.

So I called David. He was a man I knew from ACA, who was also a recovering alcoholic. He and I had been in the men's therapy group together, and I had developed a lot of trust in him. Also—physically David was a very large and imposing person, and I knew that factor would be important for what I had in mind.

I told him what I was thinking of doing, and David agreed to meet me at my apartment to help. I had decided to try another Gestalt exercise, to see if that inner child part of me would come out and tell me the rest of what happened. I needed to feel extra safe for that to happen. So I wanted someone big and safe there. On some level, Little Danny had to know there was someone present who was big enough to stop Daddy from hurting him. I knew David could represent that.

David came over to my apartment. I asked him to just sit on the couch and observe as I did the exercise, and he agreed. I placed the chairs opposite each other, sat in one, and began to speak to Danny.

"Danny, I know you're nervous and kind of scared right now. But you don't have to be. It's OK. You see David here. He and I are going to protect you and take care of you. What I need is for you to come out and tell me what happened—all of it. I know now there is more to it than we uncovered the first time, and I know it's painful to think about it. But Danny, please trust me—this is how we will begin to get free from what happened back then. Do you understand? Will you come out and talk?"

I stood up, went and sat in the other chair, and Danny began to speak almost immediately.

"I was really excited that night. I was washing dishes at the burger joint, the last load of the night. And when I saw the clock on the wall pass midnight, I knew it was January 18th, it was my birthday, and I was 17 years old. I was so proud to be seventeen. Seventeen and working—earning money. It felt really great. And I wondered if the family would do something special for my birthday." He paused for a moment, reflected, frowning. "Things hadn't been very happy at home for a while." He brightened again. "But this was my birthday, and that had always been special, so I was hoping it would be good."

I could feel myself taking a deep breath followed by a long pause, and then Little Danny continued.

"We finished work, and I headed home. Mom had let me take her car to work, so I drove right home. I pulled into the driveway, opened the garage door, pulled the car inside, got out and closed the garage door. I tried to be quiet, but not too much because it was after one o'clock by now, and I knew everyone would be asleep. I opened the house door and walked in to the darkened kitchen. I wasn't hungry, having eaten at work, so I didn't stop. I could see a light on in the den, but that was nothing unusual. Dad fell asleep in his chair sometimes, and would spend most of the night there. I would typically just walk quietly past him, and go back to my room.

"I stepped out of the darkened kitchen into the light of the den, and stopped short. I could feel myself stop breathing almost. Dad was awake, slouched in his easy chair. Not only that, he had his gun out. It was next to the chair, and he was swinging it loosely in his hand by the barrel. I was horrified to see a box of ammo, several shells spilled out, on the ottoman in front of his chair. I immediately knew the gun was loaded. I knew this rifle—I had seen him kill deer with it.

"I knew something bad, really bad, was going on. Somehow I knew it hadn't been about me—this was something going on with Dad.

"But it was about to become about me. He noticed me, turned his head and looked up at me. It was like looking at death."

I stopped—Little Danny stopped—talking, and I felt myself shudder. I couldn't talk again for a minute. Then he went on.

"I remember seeing a movie when I was really young called 'The Children of the Damned'. It scared the heck out of me, because these kids—zombies or ghouls or something—their eyes would glow and it was out of this world and totally eerie to me. Daddy's eyes didn't exactly glow like that, but they had a blankness, an emptiness that was really scary, and I felt stuck to the floor, I couldn't move. Combined with the angry, dark scowl he always had now, it terrified me like nothing else I had ever experienced from him. I felt a fluttering deep in my stomach—I was looking at death, and it had just turned its head to face me.

'Where the hell have you been?' He said it in a scratchy, lifeless kind of way, quiet and raspy. It scared me more than if he had yelled.

"I was puzzled, I was hurt. He didn't know where I had been? I would have thought he'd know where I was—at work, at my job. I said, 'I've been at my job.'"

"He looked at me really ugly for a minute, then he yelled, 'You son of a bitch. Do you think you're better than me just because you've got a job?'"

"I was terrified. I didn't know what to say. I said nothing; I was so stunned I just stood there, silent, stuck to the ground. He lurched forward but couldn't sit up in the easy chair. He sat back, then tried again and levered himself out of the chair, stood unsteadily, leaned over with his hand on the ottoman, spilling the bullets on the floor. Gradually he straightened to his full height, and he looked enormous. He walked over to me and slapped me with his right hand. A backhand, then another slap. It never occurred to me to move. To resist would make it worse, so I just stood there. My nose began to bleed. Several times as he kept slapping, I saw blood drops fling out and onto the carpet, and knew they were from me. I felt apart from it all—like I was really up next to the ceiling watching this happen to someone else. I thought to myself I was glad we had dark carpet, because it would mask the blood drops. I hoped this wouldn't go on too long. I could smell the whiskey on his breath as he leaned close to me and said, 'You little shit, I ought to kill you.' I was beyond shocked, I was numb."

"He finally stopped hitting and stood there swaying, not even looking at me, as if he had forgotten I was even there. Finally he swayed back over and flopped loosely into his easy chair, began swinging the gun by the barrel again. He looked up and said 'Get out of my sight!' "

"I was terrified, I couldn't move, but I didn't want to turn my back on him while he was holding on to the gun. I turned and slowly began to walk out of the room, listening really hard for sounds of the gun moving. I felt my shoulders tense up, felt a spot right in the middle of my back where the bullet would hit, and I couldn't breathe."

"Finally, I was out of the den, turned the corner to the bathroom, closed and locked the door. I looked in the mirror. There was blood all over my face and down onto my t-shirt. My left eye was puffed up. I looked at myself from a little apart, as if it was just another mess that needed cleaning up, like at work. I took off my shirt and threw it in the sink, began running water over it so no one would know. I took a hand towel, dipped it in the water, and began gently working the blood off my face. I looked in the mirror—saw my eyes. They looked hollow and dead. It horrified me to see myself like that. I was terrified. He could do anything. He could kill me. I knew it. My pulse quickened as I realized he could bust open the door at any moment and come in here."

"It took a long time to clean my face. Blood kept dripping from my nose. I had to hold my head back until my nose stopped bleeding. It hurt to touch my face. It was horrible, unbelievable. It felt like a nightmare. Suddenly, I turned to the toilet and threw up last night's cheeseburger. I heaved until dry and beyond. It started my nose bleeding again, so I grabbed a wad of toilet paper, held it against my nose, and sat on the floor with my head leaned back against the edge of the tub. I sat like that for a long time. Finally, my nose stopped bleeding and I started to clean myself. The t-shirt in the sink was red, so I wrung it out and threw it in the tub to clean later.

"Vaguely I realized I couldn't go to school, because my face was turning to bruises and both eyes were getting black. I threw the wash rags into the tub, ran some water over it and the t-shirt.

"I finally knew I had to leave the bathroom. I turned out the light, opened the door and peered into the hall. There was a faint glow of light around the corner from the den, but I could see no one was in the hall. I stepped to the corner, snuck a glance into the den. I could see the gun, his arm, and part of the chair, but not his face. I snuck across the hall to my room, quiet as a ghost, closed the door and got undressed. I sat there, still listening very, very intently. My room was in a direct line of sight from the den, and it would be the easiest thing in the world for him to bust open my door like he did before, take the gun and finish what he said he might do. I lay in bed, unable to sleep, aware that my Daddy wanted me dead. Somehow I knew it was because I deserved it—I don't know where that came from, but it was just there. I was terribly ashamed that I had made Daddy that mad. I got my job to make Daddy proud of me, and he hated me for it."

I felt myself come back to the moment and look around the room. David was sitting

quietly on the couch watching me. I felt totally drained. But I knew what had just been
revealed was true.

I looked at David, and said, "I'm pretty
tired. I think I need to rest. But what do you
think about what you just heard?"

David said, "As an alcoholic, I have to
say, I can absolutely see all of that happening. I think your inner child just told you the
truth."

I nodded, agreeing. "I think so, too."

I thanked David for being there for me,
and he completely understood my need to
rest. So he left, and I went and laid down for
a long time.

CHAPTER 33

I dreamed I was climbing a long, snow-covered slope. It seemed to go on forever, and I didn't think I could make it to the top. Then I started slipping and sliding back down. I turned on my back facing down the slope, and I felt like I was actually falling. I thought I would never stop. I finally dug in my heels and stopped. I looked back up the slope and it was almost flat. I was confused.

I was inside a house, and watching it for someone—I wasn't sure who. It was a long, low rambling house away from other houses, very isolated. There was a pet tiger in the house. The owner, an unidentified male, said the tiger wouldn't bite, but the tiger became startled and started chewing my arm. I would feel the size of his teeth, the strength of his jaw. I was very scared. The owner left and put me in charge of the house and of the tiger.

Suddenly, Rebecca was there, a woman I knew from ACA. I felt like she was a stranger—like she didn't know who I was any longer. I invited her into the house, and she didn't know her way around. I showed her to the bathroom. Suddenly I remembered that strangers startled the tiger. Then the tiger was there and he was chewing on my arm, and I feared he wouldn't stop until he ate me. And then I knew—the tiger was my rage.

The tiger dream disturbed me deeply, and I knew that I had a deep rage within me that would eventually destroy me. I feared it so much that I buried it deeply and only rarely did it surface enough to confirm that it was there. But I could tell. It was the legacy of anger my Dad left me. Threatening to devour all who entered—and me. Uncontrollable. I knew then that I was dangerous—to myself and others.

I had seen enough examples of my Dad's anger even after he got sober, that I knew he must have carried a deep anger like I was now uncovering. It was possible something happened to him like he did to me. I believed his many health problems were somehow related to him keeping all that anger bottled up inside him. I was convinced it had contributed to his early death. I knew I had to deal with those old feelings, or eventually they would kill me too. So whatever I was struggling with now was more and more clearly a life or death issue. In some way I just knew that I had to be willing to do whatever was necessary to heal those wounds—or those old wounds would kill me, too.

More immediately, though, I just knew I couldn't be around Wayne. I feared what I might do to him. He had slandered my integrity—tried to rob my soul. Like my Dad did. The rage was pure, deep and very frightening. I vowed to myself I would talk to Wayne only after it didn't matter any more. Only after I had released the rage, although I had no idea how that might be accomplished. If I saw him sooner, I would walk away—decline to talk with him about what happened. I vowed this to myself.

I intuitively knew I must do this. I was dangerous to myself and others because of the tiger. I feared him. He could destroy me. I had seen my Dad's tiger act out on me. His tiger had eventually destroyed him. I suddenly thought again of the movie, "Full Metal Jacket." The new recruit, Leonard, being hounded by the drill instructor. Leonard had finally snapped, killed the drill instructor, and then killed himself. I had wanted to kill my Dad, and then kill myself for wanting him dead. My self-hatred magnified itself knowing that I might even wish my father dead.

I realized rage was really not about anger. It was about fear. The appearance of strength to mask the feeling of fear. It was a paradox. There was no real power in rage. I sensed all of this, but it did me no practical good. I had a tiger to deal with, and I vowed to do so, before it ate me alive and killed me.

But how? There was the real question.

Chapter 34

A couple of nights later, I began to realize I was carrying more than just my own rage. It was time for another release exercise, I could feel it. I was willing to try anything at this point, so I decided to try something that had worked in the past. It was another one of those things that sounded terribly silly when you tried to describe it to someone, but which worked.

It was cutting cords—like umbilical cords which connected me to past generations. I knew that I possessed a fierce and deadly tiger rage of my own. I accepted that. But there was more to it—I was carrying the feelings of my parents and possibly further back than that. My ACA sponsor had called it "ancestral debts," and when he explained it to me, I intuitively knew it felt right.

"Dan, you're carrying the feelings of your parents and possibly other generations before them," he had said. "In your family, the feelings have been suppressed for several generations, and those feeling are trying to come out through you."

He had been talking about fear at the time and had suggested the cord cutting exercise. When I did it, I was surprised to see that I carried fear back to my great-grandfather on my Dad's side of the family. Doing the exercise had given me great relief, and so I knew it worked.

So now I sat in a chair and got quiet for a while. Then I began to visualize myself and my parents in the same space. I began to see if there were negative connections between us. I could see a cord, like an umbilical cord, running from my navel, back to my Mom and Dad. It was red, thick, and pulsing with energy. It was the rage cord. I saw the cord to my Dad exit from his back and go straight through to his father, just as thick and strong as the connection to me. It looked like that cord might also go back to my great-grandfather, but it was nebulous that far away. The rage cord to my Mom was just as thick, but it seemed to end right there. The way the exercise was supposed to work was to take a white light saber—like in "Star Wars," and visualize cutting through the cords several times, because they would try to grow back. But when I had done that exercise before, the image of a white light saber hadn't been enough to do the job. I had to use a white light chain saw to get the job done. It sounded silly to say it. It sounded silly to talk about doing it. I only know that is what I did—and it worked.

I got the white light chain saw and began envisioning myself cutting through the cord to Dad. The cord was about 20 inches thick, and felt more like cutting through steel. It was a long, slow process to make the final cut. I saw the cord fall limp to my Dad and back through him to my grandfather. I began to see little red tendrils of rage start to reach out from Dad's side of the cord, trying to re-attach to my side. I cut through them all again, then put tree dope on each end of the cord to seal it off. Tree dope—like I had seen my Dad use on his pecan trees once he cut off a limb, to seal up the wound, retain the sap, and keep the tree from dying. It worked before, and it seemed to work in this mental exercise—the rage cord stopped trying to re-connect after being sealed off.

I went and cut the cord to Mom. It re-sisted cutting more than Dad's, and it grew back immediately when I cut it all the way through without stopping. The tendrils kept re-attaching as quickly as I cut them, shafts of red light arcing across the cut section. I knew this cord would grow right back if I let it. I looked at Dad's cord, and I could see where tendrils were trying to break through the tree dope. I went back to Dad's cord, cut it at my end all the way through, then went three feet along the cord toward Dad, and cut all the way through the cord, leaving a three foot gap. I put tree dope on both ends, a heavy coat. I repeated the process of cut-ting a gap on Mom's cord, then doping the ends. At last I felt satisfied that the cuts would remain.

I resurfaced from the visualization to find myself once again in my apartment, feeling depleted and tired, and like I had gone somewhere far away. Yet I felt relieved. I knew now that I would only have to deal with my own rage—however that would happen. But I wouldn't have to try to release the unfelt rage of past generations, which on some level I knew I would never be able to finish.

———

I don't know if there was a connection to the cord cutting exercise, whether that freed things up in some way, but the next night, sitting on the couch at my apartment, I relived the violent incident with my Dad that I had just remembered. It was almost surrealistic how much more real it felt this time. I was sitting at my apartment, it was late at night, winter cold outside, and I gradually began to experience the events. I got cold, like I would have been leaving the hamburger joint in Oklahoma City in a car that hadn't warmed up yet, driving up the Northwest Expressway. I was sitting on the couch, and I could almost feel my right foot pushing down the accelerator, the small Pontiac Tempest station wagon responding sluggishly with its undersized engine. Suddenly I remembered the strange gear shift—a small vertical lever on the dashboard to the right of the steering wheel. I hadn't thought about that in years.

I felt myself pull up to the garage, get out and open the door—no garage door openers in those days—pull inside and shut off the engine, quickly shut the door against the bitter Oklahoma January cold. I felt the cold at a very visceral level.

I remembered opening the door from the garage into the kitchen—the little thrill of excitement I couldn't help having at the thought of something special awaiting me on my birthday. Thrilled, in spite of realizing that in our current household, the chances were very slim my birthday had been remembered, much less honored.

I remembered seeing the dim light in the den as I moved through the darkened kitchen, nothing unusual there, but then stopping short as I entered the den and saw my Dad awake—very unusual. I felt my breath stop and my pulse quicken.

I felt horrified to see the gun next to him, the bullets spilled out on the ottoman, the terrifying realization that the gun must be loaded. Now, as I sat there on my couch, suddenly I knew, I just knew, that before I had come inside, he had been contemplating suicide. The realization only escalated my horror at what had happened.

I heard the conversation with my Dad as if I was right there in the moment. His question about where I had been. I felt the shock—he didn't know where I had been. I felt my terror at the venom in his response— "Do you think you're better than me just because you've got a job?" I felt the puzzlement of not understanding the statement.

Then he stood, and my heart sank in despair. I knew I could not move, and there was no chance of escape. The hitting began, and I watched my eye focus on a blood drop-let flying from my nose into the carpet, yet also intensely more aware of the pain of the slaps, feeling the deep hatred of my father toward me, yet now simultaneously able to sort out and separate my hatred, my rage, that deep anger toward him, the deep want-ing to hurt him, to hit him, to beat him as much or more than he was beating me, yet knowing that I couldn't—he was so much bigger than me, and he was my Dad. Still a hero on some level and as the slaps slowed down, I knew on some level I would not re-taliate—which only shut the door on hope and cemented despair—this reality was all there was.

Leaving the room and feeling the spot where the bullet would hit. The shock as I looked at my bloodied and bruised face in the bathroom mirror, the almost calm and unhurried ministrations as I cleaned my face and the bloodied t-shirt.

Then sitting in my room the rest of the night, senses on high alert, hyper-vigilant to sound or vibration, wanting advance aware-ness so not to be totally shocked should the door burst open, to be faced with the gun and the shot of the final nocturnal visit. Fi-nally, somewhere around dawn the adrenalin wore off to total exhaustion, too beaten and visibly bruised to go to school, accepting that the dark night was over, that I was still alive, but now carrying the very real truth that my Dad hated me and I deserved to die, that I was not worth effort or reclamation, and the truth that the catalyst which could facilitate my immediate death would be to get a job. Dan was now self-hatred. Jobs were now blood and death. That was my truth. With the dawn I felt those thoughts slither underneath the surface of my awareness, too painful to leave in sight, yet never leaving me nonetheless. My truth—locked into my soul.

I felt myself return to the present, sitting on the couch. Once again, I was totally exhausted, wondering how long these deep rememberings would last, feeling worn out and not up to the task, but somehow knowing I must continue. I stumbled to bed and fell into a deep sleep.

Chapter 35

The next day I rested, slept a lot and worried about jobs. I still wasn't working, and money was growing increasingly scarce. I felt like I was in a double bind. I needed to work to earn money, but working brought up all of the terrifying feelings I was struggling to work through. It was a no-win situation, and I was frustrated.

So once again I drove out to Holy Name Retreat Center, hoping for a small window of peace from the turbulence and the grounding that an ACA meeting would give me. It was a rainy, cold morning.

The noon meeting was about trusting God. It was amazing how frequently the topic was about right where I was. It was led by Becky, and as she shared about her struggles to trust God. It felt like he was telling my story. I knew Becky well. She and her husband Randall had been in ACA for several years and Becky and I had once been in a therapy group together. We felt a kindred connection in some of the struggles we were going through. I saw her look over at me several times during the meeting, a question in her eyes. She could tell all was not well with Dan.

After the meeting, Becky and I started talking, and agreed to go somewhere and visit for a few minutes. We went out of the meeting room and walked down to the chapel, pleased to find it empty.

The chapel at Holy Name was one of those magical places where you felt safe— you just felt safe. It was not very large, octagonal with stained-glass windows up high on every wall. There was a very simple altar, a lectern to the left, only raised up a step from the floor, with chairs facing the altar instead of pews. Now, with the rain gently pattering on the roof, and the muted lighting, it added a soothing quality to the room.

We sat down, and I asked Becky what was going on.

"Randall is struggling, and I can't do anything about it."

I simply nodded.

"He's trying to decide what to do with his career, and it's like he's walled me out, and he won't let me help him." The words just tumbled out of her.

"What do you think you could do for him if he let you?"

"Oh, I don't know, just listen I guess." She paused. "I guess there really isn't anything I can do, but I just feel like if I was a better wife I could do a better job of being there for him."

She saw me smiling and started laughing at herself. "I know, I know, it sounds silly when I hear myself say it. But something in me is saying I'm doing something wrong and that's why he's struggling."

"Becky, isn't that a big part of the ACA struggle? Whatever was going on with our parents somehow became our fault. For me it was, if I wasn't such a bad son, my parents wouldn't be drinking and fighting." She nodded. "Becky, whatever Randall is going through is something he's got to work out—but it's not your fault that he's struggling with his career. Becky, it's not. It's just not your fault."

She reflected for a moment, she began to relax. "I get it—for now. But remind me if I start taking it on again, would you?" I agreed to do so.

"Now, what's going on with you? You looked really . . ." she thought for a moment, "turbulent, stormy today at the meeting. Not at all your usual self."

"Good radar, Becky. No, I'm not OK." I felt myself shudder. "I'm going through a lot of feelings right now." I knew the next question she'd ask. "Terror. I'm feeling a lot of terror."

"What about? Something that's happened recently?"

"No, no, not at all. I just got back a memory about some violence with my Dad when I was 17. It was some pretty bad stuff."

She looked concerned for me. "Got back a memory? How did that work? Did you just remember it one day?"

I told her that I'd had some dreams that indicated or led to something. I had done a gestalt exercise and got part of it back. Then I told her about sitting down with David in the room, and the whole memory coming out.

"Dan, that's amazing. I really hear you were ready to know what happened, the way you kept working to uncover it." She paused for a moment. "What was the memory? If you feel comfortable talking about it. I'd be honored if you would share it with me."

I thought for a moment. The memory of the violence was so vivid and awful that I had determined I would only talk about it in meetings in very general terms. To go through the whole thing would be like subjecting a whole room of people to witnessing a violent act, and that didn't feel appropriate. But I did need to talk about it, and I felt very safe with Becky.

So I told her. The late night, coming into the house, my Dad awake, the gun in hand, bullets on the ottoman. I told her about the "better than me" comment, the slaps, hits, and bloody face. I told her about leaving the room expecting the shot, looking at my bloody, battered face in the bathroom mirror, sitting in my bedroom waiting for him to finish the job. And in the telling of it, the whole thing became more real—it became more about something that had happened to me, not just something I had watched on a movie screen. It still felt bizarre, but I felt more connected to the events of that night.

Becky sat looking at me for a moment, and I thought I had gone too far; it hadn't been right to tell her and she was repulsed. Then she spoke.

"Oh, Dan, I am so sorry that happened to you. That's just horrible. No one deserves to go through that."

I nodded, feeling a bit numb.

"Aren't you mad about what happened?"

"I haven't felt that yet. So, you believe me, you believe that really happened to me?"

"No doubt in my mind. The vivid way you remember the details. I absolutely believe that happened to you. But you know what I think is going on right now?"

"What?"

"The way you told what happened was like someone would tell about a car wreck that had just happened. When they're still numb from the accident and in shock. That's the way you looked."

I nodded, thinking back to the men's therapy group David and I had been in. One of the guys would read something that had happened to him, read it very dispassionately, and the rest of the group would have the feelings. Others would feel the fear, the anger, the loss that the person reading couldn't connect to. Working through that process would help the person re-connect with their feelings. I mentioned that to Becky.

"Exactly! I know the feelings are in there. I know it. But this is such a horrifying thing to happen to someone, I suspect it will take a while for you to get to those feelings. But there's one thing I want you to hear. It's what you just told me. What happened with your Dad—it was not your fault. You didn't do anything wrong. You just happened to walk in on something going on with him, and you got drawn into it. It was not your fault."

I took a big, shuddering breath. I let it out and felt some of the tension drain from my shoulders.

"Becky, thanks for listening. That really helped me."

"Dan, I am honored that you felt safe enough with me to share it."

We stood up, hugged, and left the chapel.

Chapter 36

After talking to Becky, I came home with a whole new depth perception on what I had just remembered. The violence with my Dad was a bigger Pandora's Box than I had been able to wrap my head around. It was an extraordinarily powerful event and a turning point in my life. I understood that more clearly now. There were many elements involved—the effects of that incident spread out like a spider web in many directions. It had affected jobs and career—I could see that. Yet it had also affected deeply my relationship with God, my ability to trust God, my ability to trust other people. It had even affected my sleep patterns. For a number of years I had been unable to fall asleep at night and hadn't known why. I would lie down to sleep, suddenly pop awake at 11:00 p.m., and be awake until 3:00 a.m., on alert and not sure why. I was now certain it was because of the incident with my Dad.

I knew that it was God's will for me to walk through the feelings I had never felt late that night in 1967. It would be difficult, but I knew I had to or eventually that event would ruin my life. I didn't feel the rage; I just felt the terror. I sat on the couch in my apartment and shook with fear for a long, long time. I felt defenseless against the terror, unable to stop it, control it, avoid it. As the shaking finally began to subside, I had a new awareness. I realized that when I was in that room with my Dad, he was killing his kid—his own inner child. Once again, I realized what had happened had not been about me—but it was hard to hold on to that concept.

I suddenly knew I had another cord to cut—my connection to my Dad through shame. Somehow through that incident, I had been connected to my Dad's shame. I began to visualize an umbilical cord from my stomach to my Dad—a yellow cord, thick and strong. I could see the cord pass through my Dad, Grandpa Pat, and back to someone else behind him. I assumed it was my great-grandfather, but that figure was blurry. The image of the cord going back through the generations was clear, strong and powerful. Too powerful. I couldn't deal with all of that right now—I had to sever the connection to Dad.

I did the same thing I had done before, cutting through the cord, then cutting a second section three feet away, then putting tree dope on both ends. Light shafts of shame kept breaking through the tree dope, and I knew the cord would reconnect if I didn't do something quickly. I grew panicky. I tried to bend the stump of cord at Dad's end, but it resisted my efforts and kept refocusing on me. I despaired. I cried out, "In the name of Jesus," and Jesus was between me and the shame—it couldn't get through. He bent Dad's shame cord back on his dead body, until it lost its energy. I was awed. I sat on the couch for a long time, trying to absorb what had just happened. I felt different—more free, somehow healed. I knew for certain God had done for me what I could not do for myself. I was very clear I could never by my efforts have released myself from the weight of all of that shame. I sat stunned in wonderment.

Suddenly I realized that for many years I had emasculated God. You couldn't call on Him in a crisis, because he would be like my Dad had been for many years—He would fold up and go away emotionally—so I never called on Him believing He would really be there. As I had believed in God—He had been ineffectual, powerless. Yet from what I had just experienced, I now knew that God was immensely powerful if I trusted enough to call on Him. I sat with that awareness for a long time.

The next day I began to doubt myself and the experiences I'd been having. It was rainy outside, so I went and walked again at the Galleria and thought about all that was happening. I thought about Dad, my inner child telling me about violent incidents, dreaming of tigers, cutting cords to past generations. It

219

all sounded pretty silly walking through the mall, but it was true for me. I heard again Wayne's words, "Your friends are all concerned about you," and realized the power of that message lodged in my brain. I started to have fearful images pop into my head of Wayne calling my friends together and setting it up to have me committed. Honestly, some of the things that had been happening felt pretty crazy. I realized that—at least right now—I didn't trust some of my old friends enough to tell them what was going on with me. I felt extraordinarily alone and vulnerable. I felt terribly isolated as I walked past numerous shoppers, amid the crowd noise of the mall.

Could I tell anyone how Wayne had really been toward me? Who would believe me? It would be his word against mine, and it felt like he was the one with all the power. He had money. The feeling was—no money, you die. Wayne was Dad—the one with all the power, the adult who would be believed. Who would believe Wayne would be so verbally hurtful to me? Who would believe my Dad hit me? Both things happened behind closed doors, with no witnesses. So now some of my old friends might not be safe, if they listened to and believed Wayne. I trudged on through the mall, comforted by my anonymity and the fact that while I hid out here, no one could find me.

Chapter 37

Several days later I sat in a What-a-Burger and tried to make sense of it all. I had tried to make an appointment with Ronald Townsend, the minister I had talked to on January 11th, but had found out he was being transferred to a church in another city and wasn't taking appointments. I had made an appointment with a Catholic priest Eleanor had recommended. I went to his office, and he had someone else in with him, had obviously forgotten our appointment, and after waiting twenty minutes, I had gotten mad and left. My ACA sponsor was out of town. I had begun to feel unsafe talking to most people in ACA about what I was going through. I think what Wayne had said—the doubts he had sown about my path—had made me very leery of talking to anyone.

So I sat at What-a-Burger drinking coffee, feeling like whatever I did, I was on my own. It was late afternoon, and I could feel that sun in my eyes as I reflected on what I had done earlier in the day. I had reread my inventory work and some of notes from the past several years. It had really impressed upon me how much I had changed through doing recovery work—how much of the Dan I was before was no longer present. Recovery really had worked, and I had gotten a clear sense of that.

Suddenly I realized it felt like time for another burial. Several times in the past I had done a symbolic burial of aspects of my old self that I wanted to release. Once I had gone down to the beach in Galveston and had actually dug a hole in the ground and buried a picture of teenage Danny from my junior high annual, along with several momentos of my teenage years, in order to release that wounded teenage child. Honestly, that hadn't worked all that well, because there was much more to my wounded child and healing that part of me than a one time act could release. However, it gave some symbolic direction to the road I was trying to travel.

I had heard about burning bowl ceremonies, conducted at Holy Name Retreat Center on New Year's Eve, where people would write things about themselves they were trying to release, and burn them in the bowl as a way to signal change. I had done something similar once or twice.

As I sat and sipped my coffee, I felt that sensation again—the sense of deadness, of loss, hollowness. As well, I felt unable to continue on my own power. Since I was still unable to move on the job front, I was extremely low on money, eating poorly and not enough. It was terribly hard to try to reach out to anyone. I felt at the end of my resources—spiritually and emotionally. I didn't feel I could tell anyone where I was right now. I wasn't sure they would believe me, or they would call me insane and lock me up.

Yet I sensed myself preparing to go before an altar—to bury—what? Some part of me. In reading my journals and inventory notes, I had seen what a marvelous reclamation project by God was chronicled in those writings. I could sense all the change I had gone through. In a sense, I felt like I was about to offer myself up to God—honoring that He had purified a lot of dross from my soul. I knew clearly there was much more work to be done—in many ways I was still a mess. But it was time to honor what God had done to this point.

It was clear to me now, after remembering the violent incident with my Dad, that it was not because I was a bad person that all of that happened to me. In my mind, I could understand that. At a deeper level, I wasn't sure yet. But all of my compulsive/reactive behaviors, self-hatred, self-sabotage and inability to see or be who I was—those things were all perfectly understandable—given what I had been through.

As I gave up aspects of self-will—lifted up to God—He had removed those blemishes, healed those wounds. The scars would always be there—for remembrance—lest I forget. Yet the healing had been far beyond anything I could have envisioned. I had been blessed by God with more richness, love, freedom, awareness, faith, and courage than

I ever could have believed. What had I given up?

I went out to my car and got a notebook. As I sat there in What-a-Burger, I wrote out—not in order—167 things about me that had changed in the last four years. I later wished I had kept a copy—it was a staggering list. The thoughts and ideas for what to do with it came quickly. It needed to be a cremation—a burning bowl ceremony.

I went to the Thursday night ACA meeting and got a surprise. A woman was there from my Sunday School class, and we began talking after the meeting. I shared I had had an odd experience with Wayne. She shared how rigid and judgmental Wayne had seemed to her. She said she had never really trusted him, something felt off about him. It was a blessing to have a validation from someone who had been around him.

I came home and wrote each of the 167 changes on a small piece of paper. I used a cookie tin to receive them. I said a few words over each slip of paper, then lit it over a candle, and watched it burn up.

After I was done, I felt lighter. I went and read a book for a while, then came back and looked at the ashes. I felt ready to scatter them, so I went out in a back corner of the yard behind my apartment. It was a chilly, moonlit night, and I began to scatter the ashes on the ground, to complete the release. When I was about halfway through, I realized I wanted to at least scatter a few ashes at Holy Name to honor the significant part Holy

Name had played in how I was changing—to anchor myself to that safe place. So I saved back several small remnants of ash, went inside, and put them in an envelope.

Then I sat and reflected on what I had just done. I felt the loss. I felt the deadness. I was facing backward emotionally, so I was looking back at what was. I knew it was too soon to turn and face forward—to what was to be. But I suspected it would be magnificent—without all the weight of what I had just released. I went to bed.

The next day I went to the noon meeting at Holy Name. I was very quiet and did not share in the meeting. Afterward, I talked briefly with a young woman I knew named Julie. She was going through a lot of emotions, because her therapist had been recommending hospitalization to deal with her issues. It put me in touch with how miraculous it had been for me to go through what I'd been dealing with at home and with only the resources I'd been using. I felt blessed.

Suddenly, I could see Wayne in a whole new light—I could see his hurt inner child. I went way out back behind the building into the trees, opened the envelope I had brought, and let the remnants of ash trickle to the ground. I stood and reverently watched them as the breeze quickly began to break them up and scatter them—to release them.

I realized—I had to be able to forgive and love that part of myself that was like Wayne. I have hurt in the way Wayne hurt me. Remember. Denise. Sheila. It really happened that I hurt them. I let go of that old stuff. I could see the need to really focus on forgiving myself.

As I stood there in the middle of the tall pine trees, hearing the breeze through the branches, I felt a sense of rebirth. By letting go of so much old energy, the fear of success, freedom and fruition was more squarely faced. Had my Dad not interrupted the disease cycle to the extent he did, through sobriety—I would not have had the opportunity to interrupt the next levels of it. I had much more sense of forgiveness toward my Dad. My neck was still tight. There was still more anger, I could tell. But at least it was my anger—not the three generations of anger I had been trying to unburden.

Illusion—Wayne is an adult. Reality—see his scared child—intimidated and fearful of how I was changing—of me growing to be my own person. The same with Dad. I was reclaiming parts of me that he hadn't and it hurt—but he didn't know why. Like you did with women, visualize Wayne as a little boy. I thought of a family picture—my Dad and his brother, at around age eight, standing with their father. In that picture I could see the hurt in my Dad's eyes as a child. I thought of this new perspective as I stood there for a long, long time. Finally, I turned away, walked back to my car, and drove home.

Chapter 38

So—there had been a lot of things happening, a lot of things breaking free, a new sense of forgiveness toward Wayne, but so what. I was thinking rapidly as I walked around the neighborhood one afternoon. It was grey and cool, but not rainy—a break from recent days, so I had taken the opportunity to get out. Did all this new awareness put money in my pocket? I was stuck on the job issue, unable to look for work. I had run into Timothy after an ACA meeting recently, and he had said he might have some more painting and remodeling work soon. That felt safe—I could do that, and it would give me enough money to get by. But what about the whole larger issue about jobs and the effects of the violent incident with Dad? Where was I on all that, and how did I dig out from under all that weight? I was carrying Dad on my back still, and it was about to crush me or make me unravel.

Finally I got tired of walking and came home. I sat and shook with fear for a long time. I wondered, not for the first time, how long this would go on.

I began rereading notes from my old journals, where I'd had premonitions of beatings by Dad, but no clear images or memories. Later I realized that I had quit working in the oil and gas industry as a landman right after—within two weeks of the time when—I had started earning top wages for the industry. My decision to do that had puzzled me tremendously at the time but now made a lot more sense. I read my notes for a while longer then went to bed. Just one more connection in the bizarre career pattern.

The next day I got a real gift. I went to church and stopped by the coffee minute to chat with people. A guy I knew came up and we started talking. Donnie had been the third baseman on our men's church softball team, was in our Sunday School class, and he and I had been in a men's Bible study together. Out of the blue, he opened up and said he thought I was right on with what I was doing—going back and facing the deep pain with Dad and walking through all of that. He said I would have many gifts to share out of the work I was doing right now. He gave me a 10 out of 10 for my path. I was so stunned, I didn't know what to say. I didn't realize I had revealed that much around him or that he'd been watching that closely. I mumbled a thanks and we separated, but the reassurance I felt from his words gave me a lot of strength to continue the journey.

The next night, I lay in bed until 3 a.m. shaking with fear, unable to move. I had set up a time to meet Becky and talk after the Tuesday noon ACA meeting at Holy Name, and she left me a message that she couldn't make it. I finally moved around a bit, but felt sluggish all day.

That changed on Tuesday. I went to the meeting, and the topic was on standing up for yourself. Somehow it touched some of the anger—no, the rage.

I went out into the trees behind the Retreat Center after the meeting and yelled at God. Deep from my gut, frustration came out. I felt trapped—like I had been in the house in Oklahoma City. I had the feeling, "I'm on my own; I had to defend myself because no one else was going to!" I felt something dying in me, a resistance going away. It was time to step up to God. I started walking. I was terrified but moved slowly, purposefully. Ready to face God—kill me, abandon me, if You wish. It felt like He'd been trying. The ultimate willingness to face God. I shadowboxed with God for a long time, working out my frustration, talking to Him as I threw punches. "God—is Your will a giant guessing game? Did I not get the instruction manual on how to figure out Your will? What You want me to do? Show me a sign. Tell me where to go. I... Don't... Get... It!" I finally wound down, breathing heavily.

I sat on a bench. It felt like I understood Gary Cooper in "High Noon" a lot better: walking down that street, all alone, with no one to support him—facing the bad guys, all alone. Asking for help—why it was so hard was growing more clear. Because I did ask for help. After the gun incident with my Dad, I did cry out to God. Nothing happened, which left me with a deep-seated message— don't ask for help. It's fruitless. God's not there when you need Him. Or if He hears, He will scapegoat and punish you for talking back. His will is just that giant guessing game. The 17-year-old said, "He's killing me! Help me!" Silence. No response. That hurt more than the abuse. The apparent indifference of God. So never ask for help again. From anyone, but especially God. The thoughts flooded out after experiencing the rage at God. I knew I was hungry, angry, lonely, and tired, and it felt like God had engineered all of it to back me into a corner to learn a massive trust lesson about Him. I realized, though, that it was not my fault that I was having such difficulty trusting God. I was badly damaged as a child, so it was not that I was a bad person. I felt completely trapped and immobilized. I had nowhere to run. I knew it was about trusting God. But I felt powerless to do so. I felt strong. I felt weak. I felt embroiled in paradox.

I remembered talking with Eleanor and another woman after a meeting recently. They began talking about having suicidal thoughts, and I had gotten very uneasy while listening to them. I didn't know where I was with that whole issue now. But I felt the specter lingering in the background like a ghostly, ghastly overseer evaluating my life as it had been for twenty years, wondering when to step in and take my life from me.

Suddenly, without realizing I had done so, I stood up from the bench, and began walking, very slowly and purposefully, back inside the Retreat Center, where with very clear sense of direction I walked into the chapel. I stood there at the entrance feeling the coolness and quiet of the interior as I looked at the altar up front. I walked slowly, like a funeral march, down the aisle. I stood looking at the altar, the large cross behind it on the wall—at the space where I knew God lived. I stepped forward, in front of the altar, and lay down on the floor on my back, parallel to the altar. I lay there with my eyes open. On one hand, I knew if anyone walked in, this would look really odd. Yet somehow I knew I would not be disturbed.

I said aloud, reverently, quietly, "God, what have I not given You? What do You want from me?" I lay there for a moment, then heard myself cry out, "God, I am powerless over the self-hatred. I can't release myself from it. Help me!" I felt something shift. I didn't know what it was, but something felt different.

As I lay there, I realized how the thoughts had been connected in my head—inside the head of the deeply damaged little Danny. No wonder I'd had so little success in looking for a job. Since God was trying to kill me—He had started through my Dad, and was OK if I took my own life—why bother to look for work. I believed God was deliberately sabotaging or withholding jobs—therefore the long string of failed possibilities. For many years I had felt some deep sense of self-loathing and worthlessness. The logical conclusion I had made at 17 was that God hated me—therefore, I was not worthy to live. I realized as I lay there that much of my rage toward God was acted out self-hatred.

Then, under my shame about who I was, there had been the death wish. Logical—since God wanted me dead, to bring about my own death was only following His wishes. I felt these thoughts and beliefs rising fully to the surface where I could see them, could see how ludicrous I would find these beliefs if anyone else told me they carried them.

Yet, these beliefs were a part of me. I could feel that the disease had won—the sickness reigned supreme. I felt powerless to overcome the old beliefs. I had nothing left; I could do no more. I knew—clearly and with conviction—I knew I could not cure my brokenness. I couldn't overcome the self-hatred, the terror of jobs, the shame and self-loathing, the feeling that God hated me and wanted me dead. I lay there on the floor in the quiet chapel, feeling all of this flooding to the surface. But the beliefs felt different somehow, apart from who I was now.

Then God spoke to Danny. As I lay there, words came into my head that I knew were of God, and spoke to Danny, the damaged 17-year-old inside me. He said it was not

Danny's fault. He said Danny was a good person. He said He would take care of Danny.

And then—nothing in particular seemed to happen. No miracle healing. No lights shining down from above. No angel chorus. I was just lying on my back on the floor of a chapel, in front of the altar, feeling slightly awkward. But something had shifted. I could feel it, in some almost subconscious way.

I stood up and sat in one of the congregational chairs, and looked up at the altar. I felt lighter. Something was not there—but what had gone I could not describe. Somehow I suspected it was about that ghostly, spectral self-hatred I'd always carried. I knew it was too soon to tell for sure. But when I thought about the two women talking about suicidal thoughts, the topic no longer made me feel uneasy.

I sank down on my knees, looked up at the cross on the wall. "Thank You, Father. Even if I can't figure out what You did, I know You did something. I know You did something I couldn't do. I am ready to live, and to follow You. Tell me what You would have me do. Reveal to me Your will." I smiled, stood up, and walked out of the chapel.

Chapter 39

The next day Timothy called saying he had some work, so I began helping him with repairs on a house out in Memorial. I worked with him all week, and it kept my mind occupied and allowed all that had happened time to sink in.

By the weekend, I was tired after doing all the manual labor, but I needed to connect with someone. I went walking with Eleanor, and as I shared with her all that I had just gone through, she made a comment which affected me profoundly. She asked, "What are you going to do with it all?" She was talking about all the rich experiences I had been through, and how I had grown from them. It strengthened and echoed what Donnie had said to me after church—that I had many gifts to share out of the things I had been through. I knew some day, in some way, I was supposed to share this journey with others. I had known since I was 6 years old I was supposed to be a writer, and I had a growing conviction I knew what I was supposed to write about.

Later, while resting at home, I began to reflect on what had taken place. I still knew I felt different—changed in some subtle but substantial way. I felt an incredibly sweet and pure sense of peace. God would—and He was—taking care of me. I knew that now. I felt God's pleasure at what I was discovering. I sensed Him laughing, jumping for joy, at what I had released. Excited by the successful surgery—communing with me. I sat down and began to write.

"Dear Father,

I am so grateful. Compared to where I was after the incident with Wayne and how despairing I felt, I feel much more balanced, alive, centered and loved by You. Thank You for releasing me from so many bonds of the past recently. The need for approval, the inability to see my leadership. The new attitudes and appreciation of money—and how I was seduced by it. The reclaiming of the major incident with my Dad—where my resentment of You was intensified.

The loss of generations of rage, so much of the old anger, and the terror of standing up for myself with men. The cremation of all the old—as a reminder and symbol that You had not abandoned me and were truly with me all along. The new ability to see the inner child of other people, with compassion. The ability to stand up for myself, to take a stand, and be visible. The loss before the altar of the deep self-hatred that was the origin of the death wish and suicide thoughts revealed last fall after talking with Wayne. But most of all the humbling sense the disease had defeated me—I could go no further, I could do no more.

Through that You revealed the self-hatred and have given me back such a rich part of myself. And, I sense the ability to trust You and to receive Your love and blessings more fully than I have ever been able to do. You have given me much and have been with me always. Thank You.

The circumstances are now more uncertain and impossible—for me—than ever before in my life. No money, they are about to cut off my phone, I am still immobilized on the job issue, feeling hungry. Yet I feel so harmonious with You—balanced and peaceful. I thank You for all those circumstances. That I may know more fully and feelingly the hurts and heartaches other people endure. That I may learn to trust You more fully. That I may appreciate things like food and hunger, and having enough money for needs. But also to comprehend the feeling of being trapped and having no options.

These are such rich experiences. I see now and know now that You want me to share with others of You—in words—both written and spoken. That was what felt so odd today as I walked and talked with Eleanor. I expected to find that I felt terrified, depressed or angry. I was surprised to find myself peaceful and serene. But most of all—trusting. I was damaged a lot. It wasn't my fault. I wasn't a bad person. You weren't punishing me. But through the reclaiming and freeing of all the hard work came the deeper and more freeing ability to trust You. Not because circumstances are perfect or wonderful. But knowing of Your deep love for me. I feel so loved. With the anger and resentment, I blocked love and could not receive it. Perfect, Father, that this deep sense of peace comes when things are so unsettled. It makes it sweeter and more clearly of You. Thank You for it.

Thank you for my hunger right now.

Thank you for my money troubles right now.

Thank you that jobs haven't worked out.

Thank you that I don't have everyone's approval.

Thank you for leading me. Through the valley of the shadow of death. Through the abuse and damage—to reveal to me where it came from.

Thank you that the disease and childhood damage defeated me. That You might be glorified.

Thank you for freeing me to feel the old rage, the terror, and the anger at You.

Thank you for reconciling me to You.

Thank you for the cremation idea—as a reminder.

Thank you for breaking my isolation.

Thank you for teaching me to honor my intuition.

Thank you for showing me that I haven't messed up faith or been in a massive slip of self will. With all the childhood damage, I really have been doing my best.

Thank you for showing me false prophets and their falseness, and freeing me from that compulsion for authority figures.

Thank you for compassion toward Wayne and my Dad. I feel so blessed. Flood me with Your love. I feel more ready for it, to receive and accept it. Give me all I can take. Build my eyes to face Your light. I'm just going to sit with this a while. Be with all my friends and support them in their journey.

Continue to be with me. Enrich my sense of weakness and powerlessness, that I may access you more—and so I will not forget. I'm not sure how to ask or what to ask for. Teach me to ask boldly and trustingly. Meet my financial needs. I could use some food. Help me work through the job issue.

Father, show me a symbol of the time the disease and childhood abuse defeated me. Something that I can use as a memorial and remembrance of that time, to never lose the humility of that memory.

Love, Dan"

Suddenly I got up to go walk around and think about all of this. I went out of my apartment, started walking down the street. I wanted to think some about this concept of a sign, a symbol for when I had reached total self-defeat. I knew I wanted that reminder—something I would keep with me always. So I would never forget—never lose sight of this turning point in my life.

As I walked around the neighborhood, I was amazed at the flow of words to paper I had just experienced. I could feel the release, the shift, the loss. It was like crossing that icy creek when I had been hunting with my Dad—only I was no longer carrying his weight on my back. No, that was not exactly accurate. On some level I knew there was more to release, more to work through, it hadn't all just magically gone away. I knew I would have more feelings about my Dad and the gun—the tiger did still lurk. But I felt much lighter, more free—a big chunk of weight was gone. I knew I had lost the self-hatred that had made me suicidal. That piece I knew for sure was gone. I felt closer to God than I had in years, not feeling that He, like my Dad, hated me and wanted me dead. It felt really good, peaceful, and I was humbled by the feeling and the awareness. I walked on.

www.ingramcontent.com/pod-product-compliance
Lightning Source LLC
LaVergne TN
LVHW011346080426
835511LV00005B/150